T0311348

Using AI for Dialoguing with Texts

This concise volume offers an accessible introduction to state-of-the-art artificial intelligence (AI) language models, providing a platform for their use in textual interpretation across the humanities and social sciences.

The book outlines the affordances of new technologies for textual analysis, which has historically employed established approaches within the humanities. Neuman, Danesi, and Vilenchik argue that these different forms of analysis are indeed complementary, demonstrating the ways in which AI-based perspectives echo similar theoretical and methodological currents in traditional approaches while also offering new directions for research. The volume showcases examples from a wide range of texts, including novels, television shows, and films to illustrate the ways in which the latest AI technologies can be used for "dialoguing" with textual characters and examining textual meaning coherence.

Illuminating the potential of AI language models to both enhance and extend research on the interpretation of texts, this book will appeal to scholars interested in cognitive approaches to the humanities in such fields as literary studies, discourse analysis, media studies, film studies, psychology, and artificial intelligence.

Yair Neuman (b. 1968) is Head of the Functor Lab, Department of Cognitive and Brain Sciences, Ben-Gurion University of the Negev. He is the author of numerous papers and eight books and has a long-standing interest in interdisciplinary approaches to the interpretation of texts.

Marcel Danesi (b. 1946) is Professor Emeritus of Anthropology at the University of Toronto and the author of numerous papers and books. He has published in semiotics, linguistics, and popular culture. He is interested in the relation between sign systems and cognitive processes.

Dan Vilenchik (b. 1977) is Senior Lecturer at the School of Electrical Engineering, Ben-Gurion University of the Negev. He is interested in the development of new methodologies to enhance multidisciplinary research, with a special focus on online social networks and natural language processing.

Routledge Focus on Linguistics

For more information about this series, please visit: https://www.routledge
.com/Routledge-Focus-on-Linguistics/book-series/RFL

Using AI for Dialoguing with Texts

From Psychology to Cinema and Literature

Yair Neuman, Marcel Danesi, and Dan Vilenchik

Routledge
Taylor & Francis Group

NEW YORK AND LONDON

First published 2023
by Routledge
605 Third Avenue, New York, NY 10158

and by Routledge
4 Park Square, Milton Park, Abingdon, Oxon, OX14 4RN

Routledge is an imprint of the Taylor & Francis Group, an informa business

Library of Congress Cataloging-in-Publication Data
Names: Neuman, Yair, 1968- editor. | Danesi, Marcel, 1946- editor. | Vilenchik, Dan, 1977- editor.
Title: Using AI for dialoguing with texts: from psychology to cinema and literature/Yair Neuman, Marcel Danesi, Dan Vilenchik.
Other titles: Using artificial intelligence for dialoguing with texts
Description: New York, NY: Routledge, 2023. | Series: Routledge focus on linguistics | Includes bibliographical references and index.
Identifiers: LCCN 2022029268 (print) | LCCN 2022029269 (ebook) | ISBN 9781032363271 (hardback) | ISBN 9781003331407 (ebook)
Subjects: LCSH: Criticism–Data processing. | Literature and technology. | Artificial intelligence. | Text data mining. | Hermeneutics.
Classification: LCC PN98.E4 U85 2023 (print) | LCC PN98.E4 (ebook) | DDC 801/.95028563–dc23/eng/20220826
LC record available at https://lccn.loc.gov/2022029268
LC ebook record available at https://lccn.loc.gov/2022029269

ISBN: 978-1-032-36327-1 (hbk)
ISBN: 978-1-032-36329-5 (pbk)
ISBN: 978-1-003-33140-7 (ebk)

DOI: 10.4324/9781003331407

Typeset in Times New Roman
by Deanta Global Publishing Services, Chennai, India

Contents

Preface

Artificial intelligence (AI) is everywhere—in homes, in automobiles, in wearable devices, and so on. Strangely, AI has not made its way in any significant form into various areas of academia, especially the humanities and many human sciences (psychology, anthropology, linguistics, and others). The main reason may well be that it is seen as marginal to the conduct of research within these fields. But nothing could be further from the truth. AI is actually extremely useful in helping humanists to carry out one of their most important hermeneutic tasks—the *interpretation of texts and cultural artifacts* of various kinds. Not only can AI be applied fruitfully to text interpretation as a heuristic device, but it can also be seen to attenuate (and even eliminate) the annoying "subjectivity" that often plagues the humanities, allowing for a greater degree of objectivity in text analysis, since the computer has no interest in putting forth and promoting its own "views."

The goal of this book is to show not only how AI can be used to make hermeneutics much more efficient and less subjective but also how it unexpectedly reveals meaning patterns hidden in texts that often escape the attention of human interpreters alone. We call this "Hermeneutic AI." We will lay out the basic principles and methods behind Hermeneutic AI, illustrating its truly uncanny ability to flesh out hidden meanings with its application to texts that range from a letter by Marilyn Monroe, which she wrote while hospitalized, to the iconic fake orgasm scene in the movie *When Harry Met Sally* (1989)—a range that covers disciplines from psychology to literary and film criticism. In this realm of application, AI is no more than an instrument—literally. Johann Sebastian Bach could not possibly have created the sublime music that he did without having at his disposal the musical instruments that were invented in his time. They became the physical media through which he could express his musical imagination. Along the same lines, the recent artistic creations of Refik Anadol, such as *Melting Memories*,[1] could not have been realized without a new instrument—AI—through which the artist induces the listener to reflect musically on the meaning of memories and the ways in which they constitute our fragile identity. Inexplicably, there is still resistance to adopting "artificial instruments" within the humanities as tools for enhancing the creative and interpretive processes that are associated with texts. Our goal is to show why this attitude may be counterproductive to the very advancement of humanistic and other interpretive disciplines.

In no way do we claim that the computer is a replacement for the human mind—on the contrary, we see those who would espouse such a claim as misguided (see Roszak, 1990). Our claim is that AI is just an instrument for empowering human interpretation, especially as it is envisaged by the discipline of semiotics, which strives to answer a fundamental question: How does something mean what it means?

Current AI technologies, such as those presented, described, and used in this work, not only make text interpretation more objective but also open up new vistas showing what texts (dialogues, conversations, etc.) tell us about their creators. This is an exceptional claim that requires exceptional evidence. We aim to provide such evidence in this book via illustrations which show that AI allows for a deep reading of texts by turning them into virtual dialogues—hence the title of this book being *Using AI for Dialoguing with Texts*. Emphasizing the potential of such technology, we invite the reader to engage in a conversation (*con* + *versare*) with our own text, which is all about minds coming together.

Note

1 See https://refikanadol.com/works/melting-memories

Reference

Roszak, T. (1990). *The Gendered Atom*. Newburyport: Red Wheel.

Acknowledgments

The authors would like to thank Elysse Preposi for her friendly editorial work and Hazel Bird for her professional copyediting of the book.

1   What Is a Text?

The Basics of Texts

The study of texts goes back to antiquity, starting with Aristotle, who called it "hermeneutics" in his *Peri Hermeneias*, translated into Latin as *De Interpretatione* and later into English as *On Interpretation* (Aristotle 350 BCE [2016]). For the Greek philosopher, the goal of texts was to explain the meanings of complex things, from mathematics and physics to the workings of logic. In the medieval period, hermeneutics implied the interpretation of sacred scripture (Grondin 1994: 21)—an approach that can be traced initially to Saint Augustine of Hippo (Deely 2001). Starting in the nineteenth century, the hermeneutic approach to text analysis surfaced in the writings of philosophers Friedrich Schleiermacher, Wilhelm Dilthey, Martin Heidegger, and Hans-Georg Gadamer, among others (Seebohm 2007, Zimmerman 2015). In the same time frame, the term was applied to the analysis of literary texts—where hermeneutics remains central to this day. In modern times, the notion of texts has been expanded considerably within the humanities, philosophy, and even science (Popper 1972).

In semiotics, the science of signs, the hermeneutic approach consists in considering the relations among the individual sign structures—words, visual images, and so on—that make up a text. For instance, the word *cat*, which refers to a type of mammal, assumes a textual or composite meaning in relation to other words in a sentence, such as *Cats are really friendly companions*. Sentences, stories, utterances, drawings, myths, paintings, films, websites, scientific theories, and mathematical proofs all involve textualized (compositional) meaning. The compositional process, however, is hardly random; it is based on a code (or codes)—a system of specific signs and sign structures. The language code, for example, involves rules of combination (grammar), rules of vocabulary, and so on. In the sentence above, the individual words—*cats, are, really, friendly, companions*—have been combined according to English grammar. A sentence can be called a

DOI: 10.4324/9781003331407-1

"smaller" text, constituting minimal composite meaning. On the other hand, a novel is a "larger" text—its meanings are determined by mapping the language code used against the events portrayed in some sequence, again in a composite manner.

Overall, we "understand" a sentence, a novel, a style of clothing, and so on, not in terms of its constituent sign elements but in terms of how it has been put together to produce a composite "meaning"—a key term to which we will return subsequently. Conversations and dialogues are the texts that are of particular interest to this book. Each part of a dialogical back-and-forth is shaped by unconscious codes (at different levels, from the structural to the social). Without these, conversations would be literally meaningless. This view was put forward concretely in the 1920s by the Russian literary critic Mikhail Bakhtin (1981), who anticipated many key notions of current textual theory and whose ideas are particularly useful for the present purpose. One of these is that a text often makes allusions to previous texts—a process later called "intertextuality" (e.g., Kristeva 1980). A discourse text is thus the result of authors absorbing and transforming other texts into their own textual compositions. Intertextuality can also be conscious, such as in the use of citations and references in academic and scientific writing. In effect, a text is constructed through an interweaving of other texts, either implicitly or explicitly, within it.

The narrative text is a central target of literary semiotics, as Vladimir Propp (1928) cogently argued with his analysis of Russian folktales. In these, the relevant code consists of a small set of narrative units, which he called "narremes," that are essentially psychological oppositions (*good* vs. *evil*, *natural* vs. *supernatural*, etc.) that allow us to extract a meaning or intent from a text—an approach pursued later by Algirdas J. Greimas (1966, 1970). For instance, in a modern-day story, such as a *Star Wars* episode, a James Bond movie, or a Harry Potter novel, the overall structure of the narrative typically unfolds as shown in Figure 1.1 (Danesi 2020).

In a mystery novel, the subject, or hero, may have several enemies, all of whom function as a single opponent. In a love story, a male paramour may function as both object and seeker. Each character in a narrative is thus a sign standing for some human quality, idea, emotion, need, or personality type. Now, for the purposes of AI analysis, what counts is that the narrative code leaves semantic–conceptual traces within a deep semiotic network underlying it—a network that enfolds how sign structures are related to each other compositionally. Bakhtin (1984) claimed that a novel, unlike sermons, for example, makes it possible for readers to enter into a silent dialogue with the author, coming out of it transformed. It gives voice to different characters (in the novel itself) (Bakhtin 1984), producing an inner dialogue that he called "polyphonic." As we shall see, this inner dialogue is

In the story, there is …

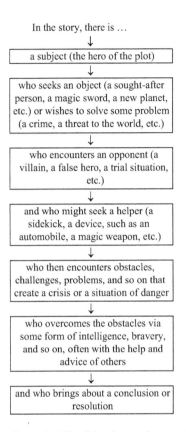

Figure 1.1 Traditional narrative structure

ensconced in networks of meaning that AI can extract and utilize for inter-pretive purposes.

The notion of a code is a key one and thus requires further commen-tary here. In semiotics, it is defined generically as the organizing sign grid that allows for the construction of texts. Words in isolation are virtually meaningless outside of a purely referential function (naming things, as in a dictionary). It is when they are combined via a code or set of codes—phono-logical, grammatical, semantic, pragmatic, and so on—that they can be used to produce meaningful texts for communication, expression, understand-ing, commentary, and so on. Similarly, single musical notes are meaning-less in themselves; they take on aesthetic meaning when they are combined according to specific codes, such as the melodic code, the harmonic code, the rhythmic code, and so on. Codes in themselves have no meaning. They provide the structures required to make meaning—one of the most basic of all human intellectual functions.

The Standing for Principle

A key notion of semiotic analysis is encapsulated in the "standing for principle" (SFP), which states simply that "a [sign] form stands for something other than itself in some way" (Danesi 2020: 473). As Alfred Korzybski (1933: 58) so famously put it, this implies that the "map is not the territory"—that is, the sign is not exactly the meaning territory for which it stands, but rather provides a map for it. When the two are one and the same, we get a tautology or a self-referential notion. The SFP applies to all texts (large and small).

Consider a singular sign form, such as the word *apple* or the word *cat*. As trivial as this may seem, it is nonetheless critical to understand that neither one is an actual "apple" or an actual "feline mammal." Words are representational "maps" that stand for something in a specific way— they exemplify the SFP in miniature. Now, when they are combined in structures such as sentences or dialogues, then the SFP involves relating them to the other sign forms, as we saw above. This principle is important not only in linguistics, psychology, and semiotics but also in AI, given that the SFP is inherent in how the elements in neural networks relate to each other.

One of the first definitions of the SFP comes from Ferdinand de Saussure (1916), who described a sign as a binary structure composed of two interrelated components—a physical component (the sign itself) and a conceptual component (what it refers to and brings to mind). Saussure termed the former part, such as the phonemes that make up the word *cat*, the "signifier," and the concept or mental image that the sign elicits (the feline animal) the "signified" (literally "that which is signified by the sign"). In effect, the parts of a sign imply each other conceptually (see Figure 1.2). So, when we use or hear a word such as *cat* (the signifier), an image of the signified (a certain type of mammal) crops up concomitantly in our minds—if we know English, of course—even if a real cat is not present for us to observe. Now, if we do come across a cat in reality, then the word we use for it (*cat*) also comes to mind. In other words, when the word *cat* is used, an image of the animal is triggered in the brain; vice versa, when we see this animal in the world (or the imagination), the word *cat* crystallizes concomitantly in the brain. The two are inextricably intertwined—one implying the other. Needless to say, wherever "cats" are not part of a culture's reality (such as in nomadic desert cultures), no signifier for them is required in the first place (since there is no signified to be encoded).

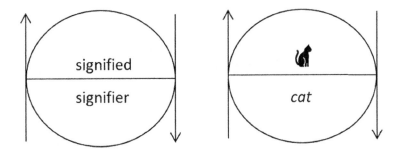

Figure 1.2 The Saussurean model of the sign

In contrast to Saussure, the American pragmatist Charles Peirce put forth a triadic model of the sign consisting of the physical sign itself (which he called the "representamen"), the referent that it encodes (the object), and the interpretation that the sign elicits or reveals (the "interpretant"). In his writings, Peirce used the word "semiosis" for the workings of the SFP among the parts in the triad. Consider again the word *cat*. It is not only a well-formed English word (the representamen) standing for a specific kind of animal (the object), but also an acknowledgment that the object has special importance to those who coined and use the word (the interpretant).

The interpretant is critical in guiding how signs are understood. In western culture, for instance, a cat is considered to be a domestic companion, among other cultural interpretants; in others, it is viewed instead as a sacred animal; and so on. Thus, while different words for *cat* might *refer* to virtually the same mammal in different cultures (no matter what name is used), the interpretant of the sign varies considerably, constituting the source of diverse modes of understanding. Moreover, unlike Saussure, who saw the sign as an arbitrary form, Peirce saw it as made to resemble its object (referent) in some way (as, for example, in onomatopoeic words such as *splash*), made to put referents in relation to each other in some way (such as in the case of arrows, which indicate direction), or else made to stand for something symbolically by convention (see Figure 1.3).

The SFP operates at various levels. For example, at a basic level, it can involve singularized sign structures, such as a single word (*cat*) or gesture (the raised thumb), that enfold a singular referent—a type of mammal, an approval signal, and so on (Sebeok and Danesi 2000). The interpretation of that sign (what it means) will vary according to culture and context, within a finite set of interpretive possibilities. More specifically, a singularized sign form can be a word, a gesture, or a symbol that has a unitary form, x, that cannot be deconstructed further in meaning and that stands for a singularized

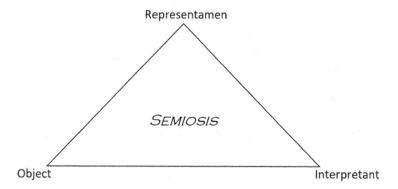

Figure 1.3 The Peircean model of the sign

referent, y (a certain mammal), but can nevertheless entail connotations, y_n: $x \rightarrow y_n$. In composite forms, which are texts of various kinds, from novels and dialogues to diagrams and theories, determining how the SFP works is much more complicated. Whereas a singularized form is one that has been made to represent a singular (unitary) referent or referential domain (even though it might involve connotations), a composite one stands for referents via the combinatory structuring of elements (Gasset 1959)—that is, it is composed of elements within it, $\{x_1, x_2, x_3 \ldots x_n\}$, that cover a larger range of meaning, with domains that nonetheless converge around a referential range with further connotative possibilities: $\{x_1, x_2, x_3 \ldots x_n\} \rightarrow \{y_1, y_2, \ldots y_n\}$.

There are two main difficulties related to composite forms, and these are especially pertinent to the purposes of this book. The first is the complexity of the meaning system produced by the SFP. No particular novel is, for example, identical to any other, given the creative permutations and combinations that may be involved in creating the textual form. As a result, extracting the meaning (or set of meanings) from a novel cannot be accomplished simply through the identification of the repeated pattern as a meaningful whole. Although the same *abstract* structure may appear in various novels, in itself this does not guarantee an interpretive constraint on the text, since a unitary meaning (or set of meanings) may or may not be inferred from reading novels. This feature allows for diversity in the textual SFP, which expands the range of meaning considerably. The different textual representations can be envisaged as "hiding" non-obvious meanings below the surface. As we shall see in this book, AI is particularly adept at fleshing these out into the textual surface.

The second difficulty involves interpretive variability. Since a text such as a novel is a representation (i.e., a map) of an unknown territory (a meaning system or domain within it), to paraphrase Korzybski, it is inevitable that various views of the same text (meaning territory) will arise—constituting a major critical activity within literary theory, semiotics, and other disciplines. This does not mean that interpretation is fully open-ended. The interpretive range of a text is constrained by its context of occurrence, the era in which it was written, the background knowledge of the reader(s), its role in society, and so on (Eco 1990). Any reading that digresses radically from this range would seem implausible. On the other hand, it is also impossible to pin down what specific set of meanings, or combinations of meanings, within the range will be plausible. The situation is further complicated by the fact that critical traditions and in-group conventions may come into play. For example, Ingmar Bergman's classic movie *The Seventh Seal* (1957) can be interpreted in various ways, including the following: (a) as the bubonic plague bringing Death into people's lives to punish wickedness; (b) as a reminder of the caducity and fragility of the human condition; (c) as a xenophobic interpretation of the plague itself as brought about by a particular group (Jews in this case); and so on. It is a matter of choice as to which one might be selected—a choice guided, for example, by critical traditions or by prejudices.

To paraphrase Umberto Eco (1990, 1992), texts are "open" to various interpretations, unless the text has been designed specifically with an intended or implied limited range, in which case it is "closed." An example of a closed text is a detective story the aim of which is to identify the culprit of a crime, even though there may be subplots and subtexts in the text itself; an open text would be a poem such as *The Waste Land* (1922) by T. S. Eliot, which can generate many interpretive reactions, even though the title itself is a guide to the "limit of interpretation" that it entails (to use Eco's notion). Any text can vacillate between openness and closedness; even a detective story will have elements in it that verge toward openness. Meaning cannot be harnessed easily; it can only be accessed from different interpretive angles.

The issue of interpretation is a key one in developing a Hermeneutic AI for text analysis. Before Eco, Bakhtin (2021) pointed out that there are "two orders" involved in any interpretive process: (a) the *experience* of something that is perceived as critical or memorable and (b) the *representation* of the experience in some composite form (linguistic, visual, etc.). The two interact constantly in generating a particular type of *response*—or, in terms of the SFP, an unconscious mapping of a meaning range. As indicated by Michael Holquist (1990: 48), in his own reading of Bakhtin, "nothing means anything until it achieves a response"—that is, until an interpretive range is evoked. Therefore, *to understand the "meaning" of a text, we should focus not on the text itself but on the response that it evokes in readers*. And this is where psychology comes into the picture as a partner with semiotics in the development of Hermeneutic AI (as we shall see).

A simple example may be used to illustrate the foregoing discussion. Giving the middle finger to someone is perceived as an insulting gesture in various cultures. Doing so, say, to a driver in the city of Naples in Italy would undoubtedly tend to evoke an angry response. In effect, the gesture, x, is a sign that stands for nothing until it evokes a response (y)—hence Bakhtin's notion that its meaning can be inferred from the response it evokes (anger), which then allows us to expand the meaning of the sign into specific domains of experience (y_n), such as the sense of humiliation, insult, and so on. The initial response implies a single interpretant, but this then involves the generation of other interpretants (which is the essence of semiosis). The gesture thus involves a complex mental representation, acquired or determined by the responses it evokes. Focusing on the response patterns to composite forms is a much more complex and open interpretive system, but the ultimate goal is the same—figuring out what something means.

It is relevant to note that the SFP does not allude to the notion of *meaning* directly. It simply indicates how sign structures evoke responses and what interpretations can be assigned to them. The word *meaning* is thus put aside in semiotics because it is a vague one, leading to logical circularities. In their key 1923 work, titled appropriately *The Meaning of Meaning*, Charles Ogden and Ivor Richards gave 23 "meanings" of the word *meaning*, showing how problematic a term it is. The SFP avoids this by formalizing how signs and texts stand for things and how this "standing for" relation produces responses, to which meanings are assigned in context. So, the "meaning" of a text can be extrapolated from the responses it elicits, which enables us to grasp how these are based on mental representations.

Peirce (1903: 231) referred to the response that a form elicits as "the set of its possible effects." It is a kind of feedback that calibrates communicative and social behavior. Showing a middle finger to another person will probably entail a negative and even aggressive response, which, in turn, may recursively shape future behavior: either avoiding the gesture or using it provocatively. This whole line of semiotic analysis begs a specific question for Hermeneutic AI: How can AI anticipate and model human responses? Consider the following text, which could easily have been found in some print newspaper or on some news website:

> A man climbed to the top of the Empire State Building in New York and jumped. He is now <MASK>

The missing word, symbolized as <MASK>, invites us to infer where the text is heading conceptually. The most likely (predictable) response is

<DEAD>—a response that comes not from the utterance in itself but from real-world knowledge (Bakhtin's experience level) that is projected onto the utterance. Unless someone has superhuman powers (as in fiction), we can assume with a high degree of probability that a human being who jumps from the top of the Empire State Building is probably going to die. This knowledge is what guides future behaviors, such as staying inside a burning skyscraper, knowing that to jump from a window on the top floor would be likely to produce the <DEAD> response, whereas staying inside as the fire burns presents a better probability of survival (albeit not a certain one).

The Role of Context

The notion of *context* is a key aspect of hermeneutic analysis. As a simple example, consider the sentence *The pig is ready to eat*. The word *pig* in the sentence will vary in meaning according to who, where, or why it is uttered: (1) it can refer to the actual animal called a pig if uttered, say, by a farmer at feeding time as he comments that a certain pig in a pigsty is hungry and is thus *ready to eat*; (2) it can refer to a cooked pig that is *ready to eat* (to be eaten), if uttered by someone who has prepared a meal and is announcing this fact to their guests; or (3) it can refer to a person who appears gluttonous and overanxiously *ready to eat*, if uttered by an observer who interprets the person's behavior and facial expressions in this way. By observing the responses to the sentence in a specific context, we can glean the essential meaning of the sentence. Responses such as these thus provide a *context for anticipation*—that is, once we know how contextual features evoke responses, which guide interpretations, we can map this knowledge onto unfamiliar or novel domains of experience. For example, when a person reads a novel, dramatic tension typically builds up in them in anticipation of a character's next move in the narrative; in SFP terms, this relation between reader and text implies an "in-between" process—that is, an unconscious understanding of how the move relates to something pre-existing in the reader's mind that is instigated by the context provided by the narrative text itself.

This does not imply that the reader is not involved consciously in an act of interpretation. It simply suggests how the reader gleans meaning from a text (or part of a text). In actual fact, a composite form will produce a vast array of responses, from simple behavioral ones to complex and unconscious aesthetic ones—all of which involve the ingrained sense of *anticipatory contexts*, which are mapped onto a specific reading of an unfamiliar text, whether culturally coded or highly subjective. The various potential results of such mappings (interpretations that are guided by anticipatory contextualizations) are, however, vacuous unless the mapping is justifiable or plausible (as discussed above). There are, of course, various degrees of freedom built into the interpretation process, but, as Eco and others have demonstrated, these fall within a range that is itself subject to limits.

As José Ortega y Gasset (1959) aptly observed, an utterance (a composite form) is both "deficient," in the sense that it conveys less than it wishes to convey, and "exuberant," in the sense that it ends up saying something more than what was initially intended. These outcomes cannot be controlled, only anticipated in terms of the contexts in which an utterance is implanted. Consider coming across a discarded empty beer can on a city street. We would no doubt read it as a piece of garbage or rubbish. This is, however, a deficient reading, since it does not take into account how the beer can got there—it could have been dropped inadvertently by someone, it could have been thrown from somewhere else during a conflict, and so on. Now, if we saw the very same object on a pedestal, displayed in an art gallery, "signed" by some artist, and given a title such as *Waste*, then we would interpret its meaning in a vastly different way. We would, in fact, be inclined to interpret it as an artistic text, decrying a throw-away or materialistic society. These meanings are based on an "art gallery code" which states that anything within a gallery is art, no matter what we may think of it. These are exuberant meanings. A test that this is so is simply to show the displayed beer can to a child who does not yet possess the art gallery code. Not only would the child be unaware of the meaning, but they would also likely be perplexed after being told what it was.

In effect, the SFP almost always involves an interpretive quantum leap, so to speak, because of the "difficulty of reading" (Gasset 1959), which tends to produce interpretive loops or even dead ends. Surprisingly, as will be discussed subsequently, advancements in AI and state-of-the-art language models give us constructive insights into what Alton Becker (1991: 34) calls "languaging," or the intuitive sense of how SFP processes unfold intuitively—wherein contexts shape and reshape how signs and sign structures are interpreted. This implies that what we call "meaning" might be a product of unconscious languaging processes (Becker 1991: 35).

Dialoguing with Texts

The notion of "dialoguing with texts" is used in this book in the sense that we are using a type of AI that will construct dialogues on the basis of one main predisposed model (i.e., the language model built into the machine) and two main inputs: (a) the text we wish to analyze and (b) prompts that we have devised to get the AI to engender a dialogical text within a contextual domain. The intent is to assay whether there are hidden meanings in the original text that can shed light on the mindset, attitudes, actions, behaviors, or personality of the text-maker. By "dialoguing with texts," Hermeneutic AI might expose a level of meaning depth that is not immediately obvious and that may have never been explored as such. The next two chapters will introduce the relevant AI notions in a non-technical manner, and the chapters after those will apply them to various well-known texts.

In this section, a general description of Hermeneutic AI is in order, so as to set the scene for the discussions and illustrations that follow. AI is a "machine learning" system that can be "trained" on large databases, such as text corpora, to extract principles of meaning composition. The large language models that we discuss and use in this book have a unique and novel modeling approach that was unfamiliar to previous generations dealing with both AI and interpretation of texts.

One of the first experimental uses of machine learning—a term put forth by Arthur Samuel in 1959—concerned computer programs that were capable of learning chess and thus playing against human experts. A famous episode in this area came in 1996 when IBM developed a chess algorithm named Deep Blue that was capable of analyzing millions of chess positions every second and of learning from the evolving configurations of the chess pieces on the board, which allowed it to adjust its program accordingly. Although it lost its first competition, to chess champion Garry Kasparov, in a rematch it defeated him soundly. In 2017, another AI system, AlphaGo, beat the world's Go champion with a creative move that was previously unknown, surprising Go experts. So, if an AI system can be devised to come up with a truly intelligent move in the game of Go, previously unknown to humans, then the question arises: Can AI perform a creative analysis of languaging processes present in texts? The answer, as we will show in this book, is yes. The basis on which Hermeneutic AI is grounded is that it can learn from huge amounts of data through deep neural networks, which are artificial networks inspired by the architecture and functions of neurons in the brain (chapter 2). Needless to say, AI is not aware of what it is doing—it *processes* not *experiences* meaning. But that is an advantage for textual analysis, since it eliminates the impulse of a human interpreter to shape the textual meaning to subjective preferences.

There are, of course, challenges to using AI in any field. For example, in the field of mathematical proof, the main challenge is that the AI does not seem to be able to reconstruct genuinely humanlike writeups on the basis of automated provers from the machine-oriented tradition. In order to be able to produce any writeups, in the past, AI had to use more restricted proof methods than those available today. But it is still challenging for the automatic prover to solve any individual problem, and indeed the program cannot solve any problems that are beyond the reach of existing provers.

Developing provers is actually the first stage of a long-term project to write a program that solves more complex problems in a "fully human" way.

Hermeneutic AI also faces challenges. But, since it does not involve logical proof systems, it has broader and more powerful applicability. It aims to decipher the responses of texts in humans—transforming experience into algorithmic process (McCormack and D'Inverno 2012).

Among the first computer scientists to tackle the problem of creativity were Allen Newell, John Shaw, and Herbert Simon, who in 1963 eliminated the wide-open meaning associated with creativity, defining it more narrowly as something that is novel and useful. So, if a computer can come up with something novel, as was the case in the Go match, then it can be designated as "creative." In our own applications of AI, it will become obvious that our system possesses algorithmic creativity.

Summary

As something standing for something else, a sign structure can take any form, as long as it does not violate the code (or codes) from which it is extracted, and as long as it conveys meaning in some recognizable (anticipatory) way. Texts are composite forms that stand for complex referential (meaning) domains. Within these domains, the referential range is delimited by *some constraints*. Now, within this range there may be "hidden signifieds" that may have escaped human attention. As in the case of the Go move devised by AlphaGo, in Hermeneutic AI the goal is to penetrate the range of meanings delineated by a text in order to see whether there is some part of the range that has been hiding (so to speak) from human awareness. It is this capacity of AI that makes it highly useful and even significant in the humanities and psychological sciences. It thus fits in perfectly as a method with the so-called digital humanities, the overall goal of which is to bridge the humanities' emphasis on human creativity in historical perspective with the tools of digital technologies.

This does not mean eliminating the traditional hermeneutic practices. On the contrary, it means incorporating them into digital formats so that they can be carried out much more effectively, free from academic biases or ideological preferences, such as those that emerged in the latter part of the twentieth century (e.g., Foucault 1972, Derrida 1978), which claim that the meaning of a text cannot be determined because it shifts according to who reads it, when it is read, and how it is valued by the society in which it exists. Every text encodes ideas that come from historical traditions, not universal truths, constituting a historically biased representation. But the historical texts are still being interpreted by anyone who reads them. And, as we shall argue throughout this book, Hermeneutic AI shows that there is indeed meaning embedded in texts—inevitably so. The experiment in the deconstruction of texts, as it is called, is ultimately useless and has failed in the humanities, although it has left some residues. As we will show in this book, there is *meaning* in human texts. The goal of the digital humanities is to show how it can be fleshed out effectively, constituting perhaps the best antidote against those who continue to deny meaning.

References

Aristotle (350 BCE [2016]). *On Interpretation*. CreateSpace.

Bakhtin, M. M. (1981). *The Dialogic Imagination*, translation by C. Emerson and M. Holquist. Austin: University of Texas Press.

Bakhtin, M. M. (1984). *Rabelais and His World*. Bloomington: Indiana University Press.

Bakhtin, M. M. (2021) *Toward a Philosophy of the Act*, translation and notes by V. Liapunov and M. Holquist. Austin: University of Texas Press.

Becker, A. L. (1991). Language and Languaging. *Language & Communication* 11: 33–35.

Danesi, M. (2020). *The Quest for Meaning: A Guide to Semiotic Theory and Practice* (2nd ed.). Toronto: University of Toronto Press.

Deely, J. (2001). *Four Ages of Understanding: The First Postmodern Survey of Philosophy from Ancient Times to the Turn of the Twentieth Century*. Toronto: University of Toronto Press.

Derrida, J. (1978). *Writing and Difference*. Chicago: University of Chicago Press.

Eco, U. (1990). *I limiti dell'interpretazione*. Milano: Bompiani.

Eco, U. (1992) *Interpretation and Overinterpretation*. Cambridge: Cambridge University Press.

Foucault, M. (1972). *The Archeology of Knowledge*, translation by A. M. Sheridan Smith. New York: Pantheon.

Gasset, J. O. y (1959). The Difficulty of Reading. *Diogenes* 7: 1–17.

Greimas, A. J. (1966). *Sémantique structurale*. Paris: Larousse.

Greimas, A. J. (1970). *Du sens*. Paris: Seuil.

Grondin, Jean (1994). *Introduction to Philosophical Hermeneutics*. New Haven: Yale University Press.

Holquist, M. (1990). *Dialogism*. London: Routledge.

Korzybski, A. (1933) *Science and Sanity: An Introduction to Non-Aristotelian Systems and General Semantics*. Brooklyn: Institute of General Semantics.

Kristeva, J. (1980). *Desire in Language: A Semiotic Approach to Literature and Art*. New York: Columbia University Press.

McCormack, J. and D'Inverno, M. (eds.) (2012). *Computers and Creativity*. Berlin: Springer.

Ogden, C. K. and Richards, I. A. (1923). *The Meaning of Meaning*. London: Routledge and Kegan Paul.

Peirce, C. S. (1903). *Harvard Lectures on Pragmatism: Lecture V*. Manuscript. Roben Catalogue.

Popper, K. (1972). *Objective Knowledge: An Evolutionary Approach*. Oxford: Oxford University Press.

Propp, V. (1928). *Morphology of the Folktale*. Austin: University of Texas Press.

Samuel, A. (1959). Some Studies in Machine Learning Using the Game of Checkers. *IBM Journal of Research and Development* 3: 210–229.

Saussure, F. de (1916) *Cours de linguistique générale*, edited by C. Bally and A. Sechehaye. Paris: Payot.

Sebeok, T. A. and Danesi, M. (2000) *The Forms of Meaning*. Berlin: Mouton de Gruyter.

Seebohm, T. M. (2007). *Hermeneutics: Method and Methodology*. New York: Springer.

Zimmermann, J. (2015). *Hermeneutics: A Very Short Introduction*. Oxford: Oxford University Press.

2 A Friendly Introduction to Machine Learning and Deep Neural Networks

An Authorship Question

When we naively think about AI, we cannot avoid (mostly) negative images of a possible rebellion of the machine against its human creators—images formed from iconic movies such as *Blade Runner* (1982) and *The Matrix* (1999). These are products of the artistic imagination, which in these movies envisions AI as a kind of metaphor reflecting the ancient figure of the human being rebelling against God, the creator. Well, the human being is hardly a "god," and AI is not a human being, at least in terms of its "intelligence," a metaphor itself, which is not identical to human intelligence. To better understand what Hermeneutic AI is and is not, we start by presenting the idea of a deep neural network (DNN), which is a central one underlying advancements in AI, and the idea of language models—since these are applied in subsequent chapters. We do so in a simplified way, without overly watering down or downplaying the scientific and engineering aspects of these systems. Since our emphasis is pedagogical, we start with a specific example, from which a more elaborate explanation of DNN follows.

Our example concerns the question of authorship and, more precisely, Shakespeare's authorship question, which posits that someone other than William Shakespeare from Stratford-upon-Avon is responsible for the works attributed to the authorial "Shakespeare." The Wikipedia (2022) entry dismisses this theory, but, in an age of paranoid conspiracy theories—which are migrating to the mainstream media and being propagated through various kinds of media networks—the question cannot be dismissed in a cavalier fashion. After all, as argued by none other than science-fiction writer Philip K. Dick (2011), sometimes paranoia can link up with reality. We will therefore seek to resolve the authorship question, not in the traditional way by appealing to the supposed authority of experts but by using a scientifically rigorous methodology. To make things concrete, we test two competing hypotheses regarding the authorship of a specific play—*Hamlet*. The first

DOI: 10.4324/9781003331407-2

hypothesis is that the author of the play is, as historically believed, William Shakespeare, and the competing hypothesis is that the play was written instead by the dramatist Christopher Marlowe. In order to scientifically test these possibilities, we will use a benchmark of works accepted universally to have been written by either one of the two British playwrights. After all, if there is not *some agreement* about who wrote what, then uncertainty would be overwhelming, and the authorship question would become moot.

It is widely accepted that *Tamburlaine* was written by Marlowe and *The Tempest* by Shakespeare. Therefore, to resolve the authorship dispute, we start by establishing the stylistic "fingerprint" of each author on the basis of these two plays and then use this to determine whether the fingerprint characterizing *Hamlet* is more similar to the one identified in *Tamburlaine* or the one in *The Tempest*—that is, to the known fingerprints of Marlowe or Shakespeare, respectively. Identifying a stylistic fingerprint is analogous to DNA profiling, which involves using a pattern of biological tokens to identify the unique genetic identity of an individual. Similarly, a stylistic fingerprint involves using a pattern of lexical tokens and their combinations to identify the writing patterns of an individual author. In both cases, we identify a set of features, whether biological or lexical, and then use them to identify an individual. In the field of natural language processing, "tokenization" is the process by which we split a sentence, a phrase, or a text into units, such as the words that compose it. We can tokenize the plays under analysis, decomposing them into their constituent words so as to assay whether there is a distinctive stylistic fingerprint of words that differentiates the two authors (the tokens are our features in this case).

We start by identifying the most frequent words in Marlowe's versus Shakespeare's confidently accredited plays. The two most frequent words in both plays are *and* and *the*. This is not a surprising result, keeping in mind that *frequent* does not mean *informative*. Because these words are so common, they cannot be used to differentiate between the two authors. So, we turn our attention to ranking other key words that are frequently found in the plays but have some kind of informative value. As it turns out, the words *king* and *honour* are highly frequent in *Tamburlaine*, and the words *sir* and *good* in *The Tempest*. Can we use these words as tokens to establish our fingerprints? As simple tokens, these are not enough, because an author's choice of words in a specific play may be affected by contextual factors such as (a) the time period or specific phase of writing in which they carried out their creative work, (b) the genre of the play (tragedy or comedy), (c) the specific content of the play, and (d) some interfering external factor (known as contextual noise). To wit, a young Shakespeare may have used a different vocabulary than an older Shakespeare, and the same is true for the words that he may have used to express different themes in different plays. For this reason, the term "signature" may be a more appropriate one than "fingerprint" to determine the identity of an author on the basis of lexical choices. Regardless of the mitigating contextual factors influencing the author's stylistic signature, studies in stylometric authorship attribution (Koppel, Schler, and Argamon 2009) have shown that the usage patterns of even grammatical function words such as *the* and *for* are beyond conscious control and may thus be used as informative tokens or features for establishing an author's identity. Interestingly, stylometry has been successfully used most recently to identify the figures behind the QAnon conspiracy theory (OrphAnalytics 2021).

In our case in point, we will measure the relative frequencies of two specific function words—*for* and *as*—as the basis for assessing whether a play was written by Shakespeare or Marlowe. This leads us to the idea of machine learning (ML), whereby a machine (computer) is programmed according to some function/model or a statistical rule, so that a certain "output" is generated by a certain "input." The output that we would like our machine to produce relates to whether Shakespeare is the author of a given text or not. This output, signified as Y, is a binary variable characterized by one of two values: *yes* or *no*, 0 or 1. Either the play was written by Shakespeare ($Y = 1$) or not ($Y = 0$). It may be the case that the play is the result of a collaboration between Shakespeare and others; however, to make things as simple as possible, we will assume a simple binary situation— Shakespeare either is or is not the author. Because we have two "labeled" plays, whose authorship is undisputed, we can then proceed to measure the relative frequencies of the two words—our variables or features—in the plays. The results are shown in Table 2.1.

In our project, we have only two cases (in the left-hand column) in our analysis (the labeled plays), but in most ML projects it is important to use as many cases as possible—the more we have with which to "teach" the machine, the better it "learns." The middle column presents the values of the specific features or independent variables that we are using to predict our dependent variable, also called a "criterion." We use the relative frequencies of the different features to identify authorial signatures. As can be seen, the relative frequency of *for* in *The Tempest* is 0.00007, and the relative frequency of *as* in the same play is 0.000013—that is, (0.00007,

Table 2.1 Frequency results (*for, as*)

Play	X	Y (Shakespeare?)
The Tempest	(0.00007, 0.000013)	1
Tamburlaine	(0.00002, 0.000027)	0

0.000013), which are called the "weights." In the case of *Tamburlaine*, the relevant weights are (0.00002, 0.000027).

Can we truly use frequency as a means to predict something? The answer is yes, as can be seen in everyday predictions. Imagine that you are sitting in a subway train with your back against another passenger. Unwillingly, you hear him talking with a partner using words such as *Shabbat, kosher*, and *Scholl*. The use of these words is a cue that will induce us to infer that the passenger is likely to be Jewish, given their specific religious connotations. Whether he really is or not, the point is that we typically use such cues to guess someone's ethnic identity. In actual fact, it would be surprising if the speaker was not Jewish. We can strongly predict that he is, based on even the small language sample to which we have been exposed. In the thriller *The Long Drop* (Mina 2017), a similar situation unfolds. In one scene there is a successful Scottish lawyer named Dowdall who is identified as Catholic because, in his "everyday conversation," he makes reference to the concepts of souls, stains (i.e., sin), good, and evil. These are tokens that are used to construct an identity profile for the lawyer.

Deep Neural Networks

Of course, identity prediction is much more complicated than the simple use of a handful of word cues. However, a larger set of words may give us a better indication—inspiring further confidence—as to which religious class the person belongs. Now, the same prediction pattern we use commonly to assess someone's identity is used by the architecture of DNNs. While DNNs do not precisely model the human mind, there is evidence that their underlying logic is similar to that used by the brain (Goldstein et al. 2022). To apply DNN logic, we first identify the relevant features and then get the AI to associate these features with the relevant class (such as ethnic identity). The word *bus*, for instance, does not tell us whether the subject is a Christian or an Orthodox Jew. But the abovementioned tokens probably do (as discussed) and thus could (plausibly) be used to determine a stylistic signature, within a confidence level—the more tokens we have, the more confident our prediction will be. Moreover, if the prediction comes from a specific case (such as an individual making the prediction alone), the uncertainty level is high, but this can be lowered, and the confidence level made higher, by increasing the number of cases and individuals. We learn from being exposed to many cases, which then enhances our level of prediction. Similarly, for a single case, an ML model will have a low level of confidence; however, this goes up significantly with an increase in cases. For instance, to test an ML model for identifying cats as a distinct species, we would use it on a huge dataset of pictures containing images of cats and non-cats, to "teach" it to successfully differentiate between the two.

ML systems can be used to assess Y (above), given that they are simple mathematical devices (models) for generating Y from a set of input features, X. The idea is to build the "best" model for generating the desired output. In what sense is a model considered to be the "best" one? In ML, the answer is clear. The best model is the one that minimizes our prediction (classification) error by identifying the relevant features and properly using them in the model. To see what this means, consider how the inclusion of the relevant features may improve our prediction.

Modeling

Imagine a situation where you are presented with a group of 100 people and are asked to guess the favorite alcoholic beverage of each individual. To simplify the task, you are asked to guess only whether each individual's favorite beverage is beer or not. The sample is composed of Americans, for whom surveys have shown that beer is the favorite beverage in four out of ten people (McCarthy 2017). Knowing nothing about the individuals, this information induces you to assume that 40% of the individuals are beer lovers. But, since you know nothing about the individuals, your "model" has randomly generated a classification based on the input information and therefore is likely to perform no better than a random guess. However, if you are given further information, namely about the genders of the individuals in the group, then the randomness in prediction can be tamed somewhat, given a survey showing a clear gender preference, whereby more than twice as many men than women reported beer to be their favorite beverage (39% vs. 16%, respectively) (Statista 2019). Using this new information, you can now improve the reliability of your prediction by narrowing it down to guess that almost 40% of the men in the sample will favor beer. Thus, with the additional gender feature, you can build a "better" (refined) model on the basis of a simple binary feature (male vs. female). In sum, knowing more about the nature of any sample will improve the performance of a model and reduce its prediction error.

So far, we have independent variables the values of which are given for each case. We also have a dependent variable the values of which we know. So, how do we build our learning model? One such learning model, called a linear regression, was introduced in the late nineteenth century by Sir Francis Galton, who developed it by studying the correlation between the heights of adult children and their parents. Table 2.2 shows an illustrative section of Galton's original table, based on 898 cases.

Table 2.2 Age and height variables

Family	Father	Mother	Gender	Height	Children
1	78.5	67	M	73.2	4
1	78.5	67	F	69.2	4
1	78.5	67	F	69	4
1	78.5	67	F	69	4
2	75.5	66.5	M	73.5	4
2	75.5	66.5	M	72.5	4
2	75.5	66.5	F	65.5	4

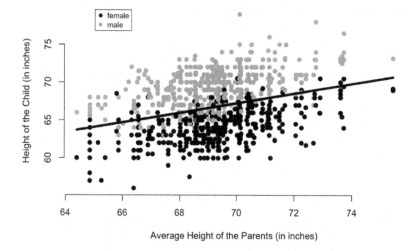

Figure 2.1 The regression line of two parents' average heights (*x*-axis) against their adult child's height (*y*-axis). Male children are light gray and female dark gray

The features in the table (columns) are:

- *Family*: The family that the child belongs to, labeled from 1 to 205.
- *Father*: The father's height, in inches.
- *Mother*: The mother's height, in inches.
- *Gender*: The gender of the child, male (M) or female (F).
- *Height*: The height of the child, in inches.
- *Children*: The number of children in the family of the child.

Now, the relevant graphical representation of the data produces the regression line (the relation between the values of one variable and the corresponding values of other variables) shown in Figure 2.1.

The function that associates the heights is linear:

$$Y = X \times b + c$$

This function predicts Y (the child's height) using one feature only, namely the parent's height (X). The function is described as linear because it produces a straight line. As a model, this implies that, for each unit of change in the X variable, there is a corresponding unit of change in the Y variable, according to the weight b, which is represented by the slope of the line/model. The parameter c is the "bias," represented by the "intercept" of the line with the y-axis, for linear functions that do not cross the origin (0,0).

The next question is how to choose the "parameters" of the model, since there are many lines that could potentially go through the cloud of points in the graph. The answer lies in an optimization function that minimizes the prediction error. In a linear regression model, the minimization of the error is measured by the overall difference squared between our prediction and the real data points. This measure is called the "mean squared error." From this we get the equation $y = 0.64 \times X + 22.64$, which tells us that, to arrive at a prediction of the child's height, we multiply the average height of the parent by 0.64 and add 22.64. In a regression problem, therefore, the relevant parameter is the residual standard error, which determines the average error of prediction. In Galton's sample, the error was about ±3.4 inches.

Now, consider the following question: What if we add the child's gender to the model? Adding this feature, we get the following new regression:

$$Y = 0.68X1 + 5.22X2 + 16.51$$

In this model, $X1$ is the average of the two parents' height, and $X2$ is the gender of the child (1 for male and 0 for female). Without going into specific computational details, the residual standard error now drops by almost 40% to ±2.17.

The rule associating the input with the output may not be represented by a linear model, and there is theoretically an infinite number of ways to generate a given output. So, how do we choose our model to resolve the authorship question? And, given our model, how do we adjust our parameters to minimize our prediction error? Luckily, we have three major advantages on our side. First, we have a set of real-world data to guide the building of the best model. This means that, instead of theoretical speculations per se, we may give the machine the freedom to identify the best model in a bottom-up manner, on the basis of the data. Second, we have given variables, and we can thus give the machine the freedom to adjust the parameters and weight the significance of each variable. We actually do not have to speculate about what different weights we should give the machine, since it can learn the weights by itself. Finally, DNNs allow us to process the data to better predict the value of *Y*, given their sophistication in processing data. So, given this background, we can now return to our original example in order to decide whether Shakespeare is the author of *Hamlet* or not.

Resolving the Authorship Question

A neural network is composed of "nodes" (artificial "neurons") and connections or arrows (artificial "synapses"). A network has a web-like structure. In our case, it looks as shown in Figure 2.2.

We can see that our two variables are represented by the first layer of nodes to the left. These input variables are decided in advance, and their values are given by each text introduced into the network. The rightmost layer has one node only, which is the dependent variable that we seek to predict. In our case, this is a binary variable—whether or not the text was written by Shakespeare (1 or 0). This will constitute the output, which is a prediction of our system and which then can be assessed against the texts

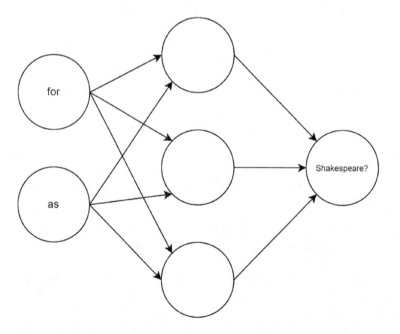

Figure 2.2 The first network structure

that are known to be by Shakespeare. The layer in between the input variables and the output variable is called the "hidden layer." In our case, we have a single hidden layer only, but, in most DNNs, such as those composing large language models, we may find as many as 38 layers. The synapses take the value of the input nodes and multiply it by some weight, *w*, which represents the strength of the connections between the units. Figure 2.3 shows the arrows from our two input units, representing the input's value multiplied by a weight.

Each "neuron" integrates the information it gets from the neurons in the previous layers—that is, its level of activation is a function of the information provided by the neurons that feed into it, the weights associated with these neurons, and the way in which all this information is integrated within the neuron's little "mind." Figure 2.4 shows how the upper node in the hidden layer integrates the weighted information it gains from the input neurons.

This then integrates the information using an activation function, *g*, as shown in Figure 2.5.

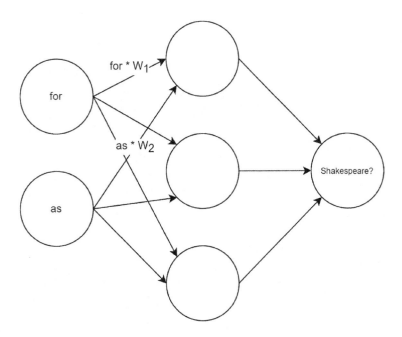

Figure 2.3 The second network structure

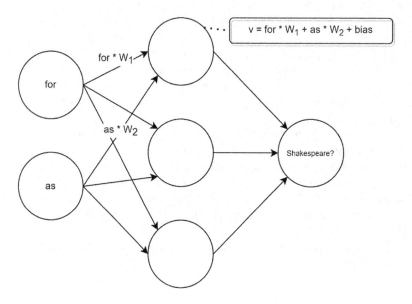

Figure 2.4 The third network structure

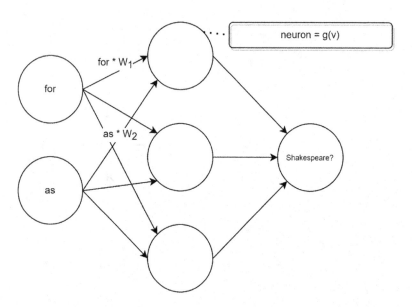

Figure 2.5 The fourth network structure

The way in which the neuron is activated depends on a chosen "activation function," which is the name used to describe the mathematical function integrating the information used in the input. There are several activation functions (ReLU), but they are beyond our present purposes—the general idea is that of input data entering the system, being integrated, and then being fed forward by a neural network to produce a number indicating the prediction that a case (a text) belongs to a certain labeled class (texts written by Shakespeare). So, in "teaching" the network to identify works written by Shakespeare, first we provide it with a set of "labeled" cases: texts labeled as written by Shakespeare or not. This form of learning is known as "supervised learning." As the input variables are determined, the network learns the parameter connections between the nodes. Each time the network is fed an example (e.g., *The Tempest*), it predicts the output (e.g., *It is Shakespeare who wrote it*), compares the prediction with the label (*It is Shakespeare who wrote it*), and computes the prediction error. The prediction error, or the gap between the prediction and the real label, provides an opportunity to adjust the parameters by using the method of "backpropagation." This is the process of moving backward in the network so as to adjust the parameters optimally in such a way that the error is minimized as much as possible. More technically, optimization is the process by which we minimize the "cost" function or the "price" that we pay for the prediction errors. For this purpose, there are now some simple and efficient optimization algorithms, such as gradient descent, through which a network may learn to adjust its weights to minimize prediction error. Using our two labeled cases with their accompanying features, a neural network may learn from the data the best function for predicting the author's identity.

To evaluate how good it is, we move from the learning to the test phase, introducing into the network texts to which it has not been exposed before, in the learning/training phases. During this test phase, the network is judged by its ability to correctly classify novel instances, and various performance measures have been developed to test how good the performance of a network is for a specific task. What makes DNNs powerful is that they can learn autonomously, no matter how complex any model or function may be.

When consciously formulating models of prediction, human beings can barely specify how they have reached their "verdict." Think, for example, about the "thin slicing" of personality, which entails an immediate and intuitive impression about a certain human being. Imagine meeting person X for the first time in your life, and based on your immediate impression you reach the conclusion that she is a crook. Trying to explain your impression is difficult if not impossible. Your brain may rely on an analysis of facial micro-expressions that are inaccessible to conscious reflection. A DNN cannot easily explain its decision either, but it is nonetheless extremely competent at learning a very complex function/model with an enormous number of features, and in some cases, such as the classification of visual images, neural networks show highly impressive accuracy.

In the above example, our model predicted that *Hamlet* was written by Shakespeare. However, the general network architecture, as described above, does not allow us to process sequences. When using words as features, we did not take into account any temporal or sequential aspect of their appearance in the text but used only their relative frequencies. However, there are DNNs specifically designed to analyze sequences, and the modern language models that we discuss and use in this book are the most sophisticated and powerful neural networks designed to analyze sequences of words. Instead of predicting a simple label, such as whether Shakespeare wrote a text, the network learns to predict the masked word in a sequence of words. These language models are presented in the next chapter.

Summary

The point of this chapter was to show that DNNs lend themselves in a concrete way to carrying out specific tasks in textual analysis—tasks that in the past were performed speculatively or on the basis of established critical traditions. DNNs are more rapid, efficient, and impersonal in fleshing out "hidden layers" of meaning in data.

The traditional study of texts and the notion of authorship within the humanities and social sciences can thus be enlarged considerably by AI, which is intrinsically connected to data science. In the 1960s, massive collections of documents were transferred to databases, enabling searches to be done efficiently by computer. Today, there is no longer any one partisan approach to AI. It has become a transdisciplinary field which, as will be argued subsequently, is highly compatible methodologically with the science of semiotics, even if the latter achieves its insights in different ways from AI. There are some very good sources for learning about DNNs, from books (e.g., Mueller and Massaron 2019) to websites (e.g., 3Blue1Brown 2022, Starmer 2022), and the reader is invited to deepen their knowledge of this fascinating topic.

References

3Blue1Brown (2022). Neural Networks. https://www.3blue1brown.com/topics/neural-networks.

Dick, P. K. (2011). *A Scanner Darkly*. Boston: Houghton Mifflin Harcourt.

Goldstein, A. et al. (2022). Shared Computational Principles for Language Processing in Humans and Deep Language Models. *Nature Neuroscience* 25(3): 369–380. https://doi.org/10.1038/s41593-022-01026-4.

Koppel, M., Schler, J., and Argamon, S. (2009). Computational methods in authorship attribution. *Journal of the American Society for information Science and Technology* 60(1): 9–26.

McCarthy, J. (2017). Beer Remains the Preferred Alcoholic Beverage in the US. Gallup. https://news.gallup.com/poll/214229/beer-remains-preferred-alcoholic -beverage.aspx.

Mina, D. (2017). *The Long Drop*. NewYork: Back Bay Books.

Mueller, J. P. and Massaron, L. (2019). *Deep Learning for Dummies*. New York: John Wiley & Sons.

OrphAnalytics (2021). *QAnon: Authorship Attribution in a Group of Six Suspects*. https://www.orphanalytics.com/en/news/whitepaper202201/OA_QAnon -whpap2022-02.pdf.

Starmer, J. (2022). StatQuest with Josh Starmer. *YouTube*. https://www.youtube.com /user/joshstarmer.

Statista (2019). Favorite Types of Alcoholic Beverages of Consumers in the United States in 2019, by Gender. https://www.statista.com/statistics/1042563/gender -preferred-alcoholic-beverages-us.

Wikipedia (2022). William Shakespeare. https://en.wikipedia.org/wiki/William _Shakespeare.

3 A Friendly Introduction to Large Language Models

Masking Tasks

Imagine that you are chatting over the phone with a friend who has just returned from a visit to London. "Whenever, I visit London," she says, "I like to eat fish and <MASK>." Because of a technical interruption, the last word is masked by noise. However, given your world knowledge, you may confidently guess that your friend was trying to say "chips"—"Whenever I visit London, I like to eat fish and chips." This remarkable ability to anticipate the next word in a sequence is built into our brains. Without such an ability, communication would be extremely difficult. The ability to guess a word is an indication that our brains constantly use contextual information to assign meaning to utterances. Following the ideas of Gregory Bateson (2000), we can think of context as a repeating pattern—that is, an interconnected set of units or tokens characterized by "redundancy." Imagine seeing just the upper part of a face, with the lower part hidden. Even without seeing it, you will undoubtedly guess that there will be a mouth below a nose in the hidden part. The ability to correctly complete the picture is made possible by the redundancy of the pattern involved, which is gained from experience with faces. Linguistic patterns are much more complex than the pattern formed by the face. In this case, our brains need to *learn* the redundancy patterns in a specific language in order to correctly guess the masked token in a sequence of words. If you had known nothing about the dishes served in England, you would not have been able to guess the missing token; this was made possible by two processes: (1) deciphering the context of words surrounding the masked word and (2) understanding statistical regularities of expression that are culturally based. Language models are designed to perform the same type of guessing on the basis of these two processes.

A simple language model may suggest, for instance, that the next token in a sequence is the most probable word *given* the previous words in the sequence. In the sentence "I like to eat fish and <MASK>," the computer

DOI: 10.4324/9781003331407-3

determines the most probable words that can fill the <MASK> slot by first accessing its "memory," which is formed on the basis of a large corpus, such as the Corpus of Contemporary American English (COCA) (Davies 2009), and then searching the entire corpus for words "collocated" right after the word *fish* within it. As it turns out, searching COCA, we identified *oil* as the word most significantly associated with *fish*. Next, if we add the word *and* to the sequence—*fish and* <MASK>—we find that the word most significantly collocated with the phrase in COCA is *wildlife*. Both of these are incorrect with respect to our sentence token. So, we will need a larger sequence of words and a more sophisticated device, a modern language model based on a neural network designed for masking tasks. From now on, we use the term Language Model (LM) to discuss the AI large language model that we use in this book.

After choosing an LM,[1] we started by entering our sequence into it:

I like to eat fish and <MASK>.

We then asked the LM to complete it. We got the following output:

I like to eat fish and I like to sleep.

This is a plausible completion, but it fails to take an important contextual feature into account, which is the friend's visit to London. So, we revised our input as follows:

Whenever I visit London, I like to eat fish and <MASK>.

This time, we got the desired output:

Whenever I visit London, I like to eat fish and chips.

The reason the output is now the correct one is because we contextualized the input by adding the city of London to it. The LM did not simply rely on collocations but took this contextual information into account. From this simple example, we can see that a language model relies not solely on collocations but also on contextual information to make its predictions.

Context, Embedding, and Collocations

Context is a term that is familiar to the humanities and social sciences (Burke 2002). Bateson (2000), a brilliant polymath who contributed to several fields of research, is one of the prominent figures who enhanced our awareness of the importance of context in carrying out meaningful communication. The notion of context is intuitively understandable but difficult to explain, and even more difficult to impart to a deep neural network in language modeling. Reductively speaking, the context is just the sequence of tokens surrounding our masked word. But this, as we have seen, is merely the tip of the iceberg because it does not take into account how this sequence of tokens is embedded in the network. One way to grasp how a neural network might process contextual information is "word embedding."

When asked what is the meaning of the word *cat*, one may consult an organized resource such as a dictionary to find out that the first definition is "a small animal with fur, four legs, a tail, and claws, usually kept as a pet or for catching mice" (*Cambridge Dictionary* 2022). This appears to be a straightforward, unequivocal way of defining the word, but it is imbued with difficulties in terms of modeling its meaning (Danesi 2003). Dictionaries are created by a collective of human experts who decide in a reflective and articulated way how to define the meanings of words. Dictionaries cannot serve as the only model of how meaning is represented by the human mind, and they certainly cannot be used exclusively for modeling meaning in computers.

To see how meaning comes about, we turn to the seminal work of linguists such as J. R. Firth (1957), who proposed colloquially that we should know a word by "the company it keeps," and Zellig Harris (1954), who suggested that words that appear in similar contexts seem to have similar meanings. If this is the case, then the meaning of a word may be represented by its neighbors. For example, to represent the meaning of *cat*, we can use COCA to identify its neighbors—the words significantly collocated with it—realizing that they will vary with regard to their "load" or strength of association. They will also vary with regard to the specific culture in which the collocations are forged. In English, the top collocated nouns found to be three places either to the right or to the left of *cat* are *dog, food, scan, mouse*, and *litter*. *Scan* is a noisy word (out of context) and is probably associated with computed tomography (CT) scans. Using the corpus of Global Web-Based English (GloWbE),[2] which covers 1.9 billion words from 20 countries, we also found that the word *dog* is more significantly associated with *cat* in Australia than in Bangladesh (2.21 vs. 0.43 per million, respectively), and that the association between *cat* and *mouse* is more pronounced in England than in Australia (0.70 vs. 0.48 per million, respectively). This is an important finding, showing that collocations are culturally sensitive.

Vector Space Models of Semantics

Useful models for identifying masked words are the so-called vector space models of semantics (Turney and Pantel 2010), which portray the meaning

Table 3.1 Vector representations

	Cat	Dog
Dog	5.50	5.16
Cat	6.32	5.50
Mouse	6.67	0
Food	3.68	3.18

of a target word as occurring in a "vector" space—that is, a simple array of words significantly collocated with our target word in a given corpus—and the extent to which they are associated with it. So, Table 3.1 represents the imaginary vectors of *cat* and *dog* using four words only: *dog, cat, mouse,* and *food*.

For each word, we now have a fixed-length representation (a vector) that may be imagined as a point in a semantic space, where the coordinates or dimensions are the words composing the vector.

We can visualize the meanings of words more easily by using a two-dimensional space in which each dimension is made up of one word only. For example, let us represent the meanings of *hamburger, hotdog,* and *pizza* using two dimensions: *ketchup* and *cheese*. Using COCA, we can measure the extent to which each of our three target words is collocated with *ketchup* or *pizza*. The values in Figure 3.1 emerged from our COCA search.

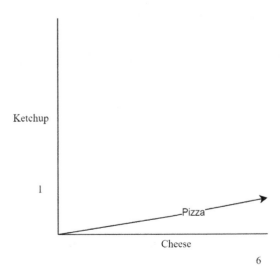

Figure 3.1 The vectorial representation of *pizza*

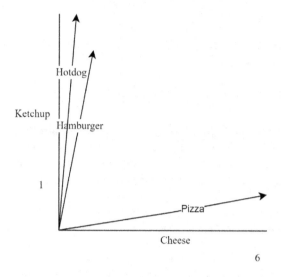

Figure 3.2 The vectorial meanings of *hamburger* and *hotdog*

As can be seen, the two collocates—*ketchup* and *cheese*—enclose a two-dimensional space. *Pizza* appeared with *ketchup* only once and with *cheese* six times. Its vectorial representation is thus determined by the value of the two coordinates 1 and 6. In Figure 3.1, the represented meaning of *pizza* is its locus as a point in the semantic space, which is (6, 1), where 6 is the value of *pizza* on the *x* dimension and 1 is its value on the *y* dimension. While it would be well beyond the present purposes, this graphic model could be extended with *pizza* represented as a point in a space with 500 dimensions or more. Now, let us add *hamburger* and *hotdog* to the space, as shown in Figure 3.2.

Both these items show relatively low associations with *cheese* but stronger ones with *ketchup*. If we examine the angle between the vectors of *hamburger* and *hotdog*, we can see that it is much smaller than the one between the vectors of *hamburger* and *pizza* or *hotdog* and *pizza*. This means that *hamburger* and *hotdog* have stronger "semantic similarity" than *hamburger* and *pizza*.

This is a general characterization of "word embedding" and shows that it is not random, but constrained by the semantic similarity between words. Now, we can use this model to guess the masked token in the following sentence:

My favorite pizza topping is <MASK> and olives.

A very large number of words could be imagined as potential candidates for the missing slot. However, we can now expect, with a high degree of assurance, that it is words that have a high semantic similarity with *pizza*, *topping*, and *olives* that will be the best fit. One of these is *cheese*.

The notion of embedding involves the collocation of words in a vectorial space (Turney and Pantel 2010). Embedding is therefore a contextual representation of meaning via the association of the target word with other words that appear with it in the same lexical–semantic environment. It is an "a-temporal" form of representation that is indifferent to the position of the word in the sentence but sensitive to the specific corpus from which it has been extracted. Different corpora may lead to different representations. When a sequence of tokens (words) enters the LM, it is first encoded (represented) as a sequence of vectors. The encoder's task is to provide a relevant and rich representation of the sequence that can then be easily processed by the computer's algorithm.[3] Put differently, the encoder gets as an input a sequence of words, which it then generates as a sequence of embeddings (vectors).

Why is this so important for a contextual representation? Consider the example we previously used. When forming the embedding of *London* and *eat*, we may find that *London* is a context where one of the preferred dishes eaten by tourists is represented by the collocation *fish* and *chips*. The embedding of *London* and *eat* will therefore provide a context in which the masked word following *fish and* is *chips*, with a very high probability. In effect, the context is not only the words in the sequence preceding our masked token but also their embedding structure. However, not all words are born equal, and some of them are more informative than others. Here, the concept of *attention* (Lindsay 2020) comes into play, which involves fine tuning the context in the sense that the representation of each token in the sequence is adjusted to take account of the representation of the other tokens.

Attention Mechanisms

Generally described, attention is a process through which we select which stimuli to focus on or to be in tune with. As you read this book, your attention is hopefully given to the text rather than to other interfering stimuli, from a yawning cat to the rain falling outside. So, attention concerns *ignoring* some data and being attuned to other more relevant data. Ignoring and attuning are complementary processes. When we try to predict a masked word, we give our attention to more informative words such as *London* rather than to less informative words such as *like*. This may sound like common sense, but it is far from trivial to understand how we direct our attention to relevant pieces of information in a statement and even less trivial to design an attention mechanism for a neural network.

An interesting explanation of the attention factor (Radulescu et al. 2021) involves the role of natural regularities and statistical inference. In contrast to the idea that all knowledge is innate, we know today that we learn by building statistical models of regularities in a developmentally incremental way. Knowledge is gained from the experiences of generations of human beings, encoded in mental mechanisms that predict regularities and patterns in information. Our brains have also developed mechanisms of attention, which are activated spontaneously. In language, these are involved in deciphering the role of relevant words in a sequence by unconsciously identifying statistical regularities within the sequence, as well as by applying the contextualized knowledge of the world we have acquired through years of learning and personal development. These are the relevant parameters in decoding meaning. Similarly, neural networks learn to optimize adjustments of the parameters for a specific task. The design of modern language models is in principle no different from the design of our brains; however, instead of allowing the machine to naturally evolve over generations, we intervene in the machine's learning system with a huge number of textual sequences, thus shortening its learning rate.

How does it actually work? The attention mechanism assumes that some words are more important than others. However, as the embedding associated with each word is fixed and determined in advance, the values that appear in the vector space are not context sensitive, and so the LM must re-weight each vector. First, we use the sequence of tokens and map them into vectors. For example, the sequence "Whenever I visit London, I like to eat fish and <MASK>" can be mapped into a sequence of vectors (embeddings), as shown in Table 3.2.

Next, we use a set of weights to get a new set of better vectors in the sense that they are designed to be context sensitive. Let us see how this works by examining the vectors for *London, eat,* and *fish* (see Figure 3.3).

Table 3.2 Vectors

Word	Vector
Whenever	V_1
I	V_2
visit	V_3
London	V_4
...	V_5
and	V_n

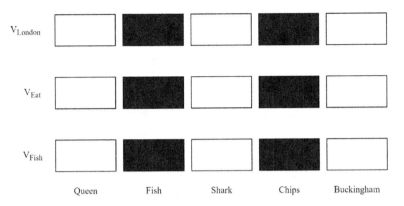

Figure 3.3 The vectorial representation (i.e., embedding) of the words *London*, *eat*, and *fish*

We notice that the vectors share some similarities (marked by the black rectangles). The words *Queen* and *Buckingham* may be strongly represented in the embedding of *London*, but they have nothing to do with *fish*. While *shark* is a word strongly associated with *fish*, it also has no relevance to our case. To re-weight each vector, we simply form a new weight by multiplying each vector by each other vector:

$$V_{London} \times V_{London} = W_{11}$$

$$V_{London} \times V_{Eat} = W_{12}$$

$$V_{London} \times V_{Fish} = W_{13}$$

Normalizing the weights into a range of 0–1, we get a single number indicating the extent to which the vectors are similar. For *London* it is as follows:

$$y1 = V_{London} \times W_{11} + V_{Eat} \times W_{12} + V_{Fish} \times W_{13}$$

This can be made more concrete by using a biased example. To do so, we represent the vectors of *London*, *eat*, and *fish* in terms of two dimensions only: *Queen* and *chips* (see Table 3.3).

Table 3.3 Vectors

	V_{London}	V_{Eat}	V_{Fish}
Queen	9	2	1
Chips	1	8	9

The weights are calculated as the "dot products" of the vectors:

$$V_{London} \times V_{London} = W_{11} = 82$$

$$V_{London} \times V_{Eat} = W_{12} = 26$$

$$V_{London} \times V_{Fish} = W_{13} = 18$$

The new vector, y, is a transformed and context-sensitive version of V_{London}, with the vector values normalized to percentages. The old embedding of *London* gave 90% importance to the token/word *Queen* and only 10% importance to the token/word *chips*. However, the new vector y decreases the importance of *Queen* to 65% and increases the importance of *chips* to 35%. This mechanism is called "self-attention," since it has moved the vector of *London* closer to the vector of *fish*.

When performing this re-weighting, we give more weight to the "shared context" of the words in the vectors. Multiplying the embedding of *London* by the embedding of *eat*, for instance, would emphasize the context of *eating in London*, and this weight is used to re-weight the vector of *eat*, which is in turn used to adjust the vector of *London*. This mechanism of self-attention clearly improves the contextual representation of words. The first context was formed by representing each word through embedding, and the second one by self-attention, through which the embedding of each word becomes more sensitive to the context of the other words.

In sum, concerning an utterance such as "Whenever I visit London, I like to eat fish and <MASK>," a well-trained LM possesses all the mechanisms necessary to guess the masked word. It may turn out that the friend actually intended a different word than *chips*, but their intended word might have a very low probability. Some guesses or outputs may be more likely than others, but the LM's degrees of freedom in guessing the next token are constrained by the same kinds of contextual factors as those possessed by the human brain.

LMs process all tokens simultaneously, producing "position embeddings"—the positions of the tokens in the sequence. Position embedding provides another (third) dimension of contextualization. It implies that we do not only represent the meanings of words through embedding and adjust their sensitivity to the words in their immediate surroundings, but that we also take the temporal dimension or "contextual positioning" into account.

Now, what does it really mean to say that LMs "learn" from data? Let us consider our example again. Each vector is fed into a neural network called a linear layer. Figure 3.4 shows the (transformed) embedding of *London* as a three-dimensional input including the words *Queen*, *fish*, and *chips*.

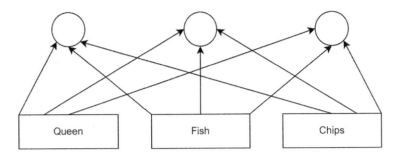

Figure 3.4 Feeding the linear layer

This network will produce an output as another vector but of a lower dimensionality. The actual LM has three separate linear layers corresponding to different functions. The vectors are used as inputs to the three layers in such a way that a better representation of the vector is possible. The LM also uses a mechanism called "multi-head" attention, whereby several attention-based procedures are enlisted to produce a final output. What is "learned" through the use of these multiple layers of neural networks is the weights that are best associated with the components of a vector, but this is not all that is involved. Recall the Shakespeare authorship question (chapter 2). When we tried to teach the computer to identify the textual signature of Shakespeare, we actually "taught" it to successfully perform a classification task based on the "features" that identify a text as written by Shakespeare or not. Analogously, when trained to identify a masked word, the LM actually learns to identify the words that are most likely to fit into the missing slot in the text.

During the training phase, the LM is exposed to sequences with masked words and their "solutions." No "labeling" of the data by human beings is required. Consider the following three sentences:

1. "I got into the bathroom and washed my <MASK> [face]."
2. "Gin and <MASK> [tonic] is usually served cold."
3. "To prepare pizza you need the following ingredients: flour, <MASK> [cheese], tomato, yeast, water, and salt."

As the LM observes *numerous* examples such as these, it learns how to adjust its representations to best identify the masked words. We emphasize "numerous" because modern language models are based on huge amounts of data—hence their designation as "large language models."

In practice, the LM uses as a context all of the words that appear in the sequence. Previously, we have shown how including reference to the city *London* led to the best answer. Here is the fourth and final contextual dimension of the LM—attuning to a criterion. The criterion is the success of the network in identifying the masked token. For example, the sentence

>   I <MASK> people who offend me.

might be completed by negatively loaded words such as *hate*. But what if the following context is added to the sentence?

>   As a devoted Christian taught to turn the other cheek, I <MASK> people who offend me.

With this contextual input, an LM trained to "learn" against a criterion (a mask word) will favor more positive words, such as *forgive*.

Summary

Large language models (e.g., Vaswani et al. 2017) are neural network architectures that are designed with highly sophisticated context-sensitive mechanisms for word representation and that are trained to identify a masked token. Given their unique architecture, the models can be used for sequence and text generation, which is an extension of their ability to successfully identify a masked token. These models are called "general" because they are trained on a huge dataset of texts, but they may sometimes be optimized for a given task by fine tuning them with a smaller corpus. For instance, in modeling the psychopathic mind, it is possible to use a general language model but fine-tune the model by using a small set of texts produced by fictive psychopathic characters (Neuman, Vilenchik, and Kozhakuv 2022). It is important to remember, though, that LMs are not substitutes for the human mind. To reiterate here, computers are *processors*, not *interpreters* in the human sense.

   LMs are astonishing machines, but to use them successfully one has to move from semantics to pragmatics, as discussed in this chapter, in the sense of using language "in context" (Mey 2001) and, more accurately, in a *specific context*—that is, "a large language model will only be able to tell truths about its own experience when such an experience actually exists—which, today, it does not" (Aguera y Arcas 2021). The "experience" of the LM is the textual space in which it has been trained, which is a limited context for decoding actual meaning. This is why the model sometimes generates "off-target" results, nonsense, or non sequiturs as responses. Above all else, it must be kept in mind that large language models are only tools, albeit powerful ones, as will be illustrated in the remainder of this book.

Notes

1 We use the demo of https://6b.eleuther.ai throughout the book.
2 See www.english-corpora.org/glowbe
3 For a short introduction see Rasa Learning Centre (2020).

References

Aguera y Arcas, B. (2021). Do Large Language Models Understand Us? https://medium.com/@blaisea/do-large-language-models-understand-us-6f881d6d8e75.

Bateson, G. (2000). *Steps to an Ecology of Mind: Collected Essays in Anthropology, Psychiatry, Evolution, and Epistemology*. Chicago: University of Chicago Press.

Burke, P. (2002). Context in Context. *Common Knowledge* 8: 152–177.

Cambridge Dictionary (2022). Cat. https://dictionary.cambridge.org/dictionary/english/cat.

Danesi, M. (2003). Metaphorical "Networks" and Verbal Communication: A Semiotic Perspective of Human Discourse. *Σημειωτκή: Sign Systems Studies* 31: 341–364.

Davies, M. (2009). The 385+ Million Word Corpus of Contemporary American English (1990–2008+): Design, Architecture, and Linguistic Insights. *International Journal of Corpus Linguistics* 14: 159–190.

Firth, J. R. (1957). *Studies in Linguistic Analysis*. London: Wiley-Blackwell.

Harris, Z. (1954). Distributional Structure. *Word* 10: 146–162.

Lindsay, G. W. (2020). Attention in Psychology, Neuroscience, and Machine Learning. *Frontiers in Computational Neuroscience* 14. https://doi.org/10.3389/fncom.2020.00029.

Mey, J. L. (2001). *Pragmatics: An Introduction*. Oxford: Blackwell.

Neuman, Y., Vilenchik, D., and Kozhakuv, V. (2022, under review). *Data Augmentation for Modeling Human Personality: The Dexter Machine*.

Radulescu, A., Shin, Y. S., and Niv, Y. (2021). Human Representation Learning. *Annual Review of Neuroscience* 44: 253–273.

Rasa Learning Center (2020). NLP for Developers: Word Embeddings. https://learning.rasa.com/nlp-for-devs/embeddings.

Turney, P. D. and Pantel, P. (2010). From Frequency to Meaning: Vector Space Models of Semantics. *Journal of Artificial Intelligence Research* 37: 141–188.

Vaswani, A. et al. (2017). Attention Is All You Need. *Advances in Neural Information Processing Systems* 30: 5998–6008.

4 Using AI for Dialoguing with Texts

Applying AI

AI in itself cannot substitute the human interpreter, and therefore it is more accurate to say that AI is a means to augment natural intelligence with artificial systems. This chapter will present an overview of how such AI—called Hermeneutic AI—may be utilized to decipher layers of meaning in human-made texts. To do so, we will use two texts: (a) a letter written by the actress Marilyn Monroe from her bed in hospital and (b) a stretch of dialogue from the movie *Joker* (2019). Our goal here is to show how AI can enter into a communicative interaction with these texts, generating its own virtual dialogues that have unexpected implications for understanding the text and its producer.

As discussed in the opening chapter, the interpretive process is based on the SFP (standing for principle), which in the present case implies using deep neural networks (DNNs) to penetrate what the "standing for" implies beyond the normal range of signifieds or interpretants (chapter 1). The notions of DNNs (chapter 2) and modern language models (chapter 3) can now be incorporated directly into the SFP dimension of texts, with Monroe's letter constituting an initial test case for examining how they can be applied to unravel meanings beyond the surface text. The essence of Hermeneutic AI is to squeeze hidden meanings out of texts by converting the texts into virtual dialogues based on their neural network structure. To apply cybernetician J. C. Licklider's (1960) remarks to Hermeneutic AI, it can be said that it complements natural intelligence's "strengths to a high degree."

The LM described in the previous chapter does indeed augment human intelligence—not replace it—by its ability to process enormous amounts of data in order to learn from it, converting the patterns inherent in it into representations that predict new outputs from specific test cases. The goal here is to show that AI can indeed help to uncover the hidden meanings in texts, via its ability to "dialogue with the texts."

DOI: 10.4324/9781003331407-4

As discussed in the previous chapter, the LM learns how embedding is constructed from a large corpus of text. The text that is fed into the LM is the one written by the individual in question (Monroe or the Joker). We used a pre-trained LM model, which means that we did not have any control over the texts with which it had been trained. But we could prime the LM dynamically with a specific text, which it was then asked to complete. We started by prompting the LM with a text written by Monroe or associated with the Joker. This action contextualized the LM to that given text, and it then produced completions accordingly.

Marilyn Monroe's Letter

To illustrate the power of the LM to support a sophisticated textual analysis, we will first use a letter written by Marylin Monroe (1926–1962).[1] As is well known, Monroe was a Hollywood motion-picture actress whose great beauty made her a world-famous "sex symbol." But, in spite of her success in films, Monroe lived a tragic life. She died at the age of 36 from an overdose of sleeping pills. Since her death, she has become one of the most iconic figures in the history of cinema. Her troubled background and the fact that she was exploited by the men in her life turned her into a symbolic martyr standing for the sad plight of American womanhood in her era.

In 1961, Monroe suffered a serious mental breakdown, resulting in hospitalization. From her bed, she wrote a letter to her psychiatrist, which we submitted to the LM so that it could talk to Monroe via a virtual dialogue that it has the capacity to generate. When we read Monroe's actual letter, we are reading a text devised decades ago whose author died shortly after writing it, in what is officially considered to be suicide. The LM's virtual "dialoguing" method allows us to talk with its author—Monroe—virtually, as if she were alive. It is through the dialogue format that we can come to understand a text-maker, based on the DNN's ability to reconstruct meaning structures in the ways that were discussed previously.

Monroe was hospitalized after suffering through long periods of depression. Penetrating the reason for her state of mind was our premise for using the LM, which avoids the subjective problems involved in human-to-human interactions and in human interpretations of her letter. We started by considering Monroe's use of the first-person pronoun "I" in her opening sentence, which suggests that she was attempting to provide a personal perspective on her state:

Just now when I looked out the hospital window where the snow had covered everything suddenly everything is kind of a muted green.

With this sentence, Monroe locates herself—the "I"—in the particular situation of observing the outside world (the "non-I" world) from the hospital's window. The pronoun is a semiotic index—a sign that directs our attention uniquely to the author, Monroe, and her specific state of mind. As Michael Holquist (1990: 28) states: "Much as Peter Pan's shadow is sewn to his body, the 'I' is the needle that stitches the abstraction of language to the particularity of the lived experience."

To dig deeper into the meaning of Monroe's opening sentence, we got the LM to ask the text "questions" so that we could examine the "answers" that it generated. This phenomenological approach (Petitmengin, Remillieux, and Valenzuela-Moguillansky 2019) allowed us to focus initially on what the sentence conveys with regard to Monroe's inner experiences, rather than focusing directly on *how* or *why* Monroe had this experience. Monroe's opening sentence thus provides an initial context for accessing the first layer of meaning using the LM. This does not mean that the role of the human interpreter is dismissible; rather, it allows the human interpreter to formulate crucial questions, or prompts, that the LM can use to produce a revealing virtual dialogue and the hidden layers of meaning that may be in the original text.

To repeat, Monroe's opening sentence describes a personal experience (*I looked*) in synchronic time (*Just now*), and this experience is projected onto the world outside the window via synesthetic figurative language (*snow ... a muted green*). This imbues the entire first paragraph of the letter with a tinge of melancholy. We then inputted the first paragraph into the LM:[2]

Monroe: Just now when I looked out the hospital window where the snow had covered everything suddenly everything is kind of a muted green. The grass, shabby evergreen bushes—though the trees give me a little hope—the desolate bare branches promising maybe there will be spring and maybe they promise hope.
Questioner: How does it feel to be muted?

The prompt that we have designed and entered into the system as the *Questioner* is our own way of prompting the LM with the context relevant for our specific interpretative aim. The prompt aims to get our Virtual Monroe to explain herself. The ensuing text (virtual dialogue) is then automatically generated by the LM, on the basis of the LM that already exists in the network's mind (chapter 3). Following is the dialogical output:

Monroe: It's how I feel inside. (Pause)
Questioner: What's the worst thing that could happen to you?
Monroe: (Muttering to herself) I could die.

Questioner: Is that your worst fear?
Monroe: That's my worst fear. *I want to die.* (Our emphasis)

As can be seen, through our prompt, the LM exposes suicidal wishes simply by transforming the opening paragraph via a prompt into a virtual dialogical sequence. Technically, the sequence is a statistically generated one attained by running the LM repeatedly. The LM is guided by a parameter called its "temperature," which refers to the probability level of its output. The higher the temperature, the "wilder" is the generated sequence; the lower the temperature, the more likely it is. In other words, a lower temperature makes the model's output more conservative; a higher temperature makes it wilder. For our virtual dialogue, the temperature was usually set to 0.90, where the maximum level of potential energy is "1." The LM then generated another output:

Monroe: Um, I can hear the night birds but I can't see them. I can hear the wind, but I can't hear its roar. I can hear the crack of a branch, but I can't hear the trees crack. I can hear the trees, but I can't hear the wind. I can hear the wind, but I can't hear the birds. I can hear the birds but they're muted. I can hear the birds but I can't see them.
Questioner: Do you feel like you're there?
Monroe: I feel disconnected. I feel like there's this limbo.
Questioner: What kind of limbo?
Monroe: Like the leaves, they don't really know what's going on.
Questioner: How do you feel about being muted, not being in the world?
Monroe: I feel like I'm not in the world at all.
Questioner: What does that feel like?
Monroe: I feel like I'm going to die.

The virtual dialogue, *generated by the LM* through the mediation of human interpreters (i.e., the *Questioner*), has seemingly been able to penetrate the mind of Monroe—that is, it was able, virtually, to (re)construct Monroe's inner world in a way that is not apparent in the original inputted text.

The LM's (Re)construction

A key aspect of the LM's processing of the given input was that it generated consistent virtual dialogues from the same input (and prompts). Since the LM has a built-in randomness device, it is not a simple deterministic machine that generates the same output from the same input. In a similar fashion to Argentine writer Jorge Borges' *Garden of Forking Paths* ([1941] 1999), in which the same utterance leads to forking trajectories in the narrative, the LM generates "forking paths" that are critical in penetrating Monroe's state of mind. The first path (or dialogical snippet) provides us with two insights: (a) Monroe's experience of the view outside the window as *a muted green* is a mirror of her inside world ("It's how I feel inside"), rather than a form of poetic language in itself, and (b) Monroe is revealed as being depressed, which is the source of her suicidal thoughts ("I want to die"). It is important to emphasize that neither of these are expressed *explicitly* in the original text written by Monroe. The LM was thus able to flesh out from her letter the inner state of her mind, which, tragically, led subsequently to her death.

We note, further, that the morbid atmosphere identified in the first output is evident in the second output (the second path) as well ("I feel like I'm going to die"), and this is connected to a sense of emotional alienation or disconnectedness ("I feel disconnected" and "I feel like I'm not in the world at all"). By identifying this sense, the LM has given us a better understanding of the depressive state that Monroe was likely experiencing, which was a plausible source of her suicidal intentions. We have thus learned something from the LM's virtual dialogues that is certainly not trivial, given that Monroe actually ended up dying by suicide. The LM's dialogues indicate, in effect, that Monroe's letter was not a simple poetic description of what her eyes saw outside the window; rather, it was hiding beneath the surface what she was experiencing internally. We also learn via the LM that depression involves an experience of alienation with an accompanying death wish. These forking paths are not disconnected but converge, since both are connected to the painful experience produced by a deep clinical depression.

As a result of our AI "dialoguing" with Monroe's text, we are now in a better position to project its content as a warning about her future suicidal action. The inevitable question that comes to mind is whether we could get the same type of insight *without* using the AI. The answer is not clear. On the one hand an expert psychologist could have reached the same conclusions. On the other hand it is not clear whether readers of the text could have easily reached the same converging paths. All the AI did was to provide us with a tool that fleshed out of a text forking paths that converge to the same thematic point—Monroe's depression. It did so by using the LM structure implied by the specific lexico-grammatical choices of the opening paragraph, expanding on something that Monroe was afraid to acknowledge consciously—namely, that she was at a tipping point that was far beyond what she expressed in the letter. As "inputters," our task was to identify the utterances in the text that were specifically relevant to the LM in a way that would prompt the Virtual Monroe to reveal her inner pain. This led to a top–down interpretation of the text by the LM, breaking it down into its compositional forms, through which we discovered interpretive paths that would otherwise have been difficult to discern, at least methodologically and explicitly. This methodology is clearly a powerful one, constituting a first stage in dialoguing with Monroe's other texts and bridging the gap between her real experience and how she represented it. As we will see, we subsequently used the LM to go further into her mind by generating other virtual dialogues, in which various interpretive paths emerged.

The prompts devised for the LM were based on psychodynamic theory (Lingiardi et al. 2015), in which an individual's personality is seen as manifesting itself along several dimensions—beliefs about oneself, views of others, reasons for inner conflict, and emotional states—and in the coping (defense) mechanisms that the subject deploys to handle stressful situations. Specifically, the prompts were inspired by the *Psychodynamic Diagnostic Manual* (Lingiardi and McWilliams 2017), which enables clinicians to describe and categorize personality patterns, social and emotional features, personal experiences, and the like. Prompting from the psychodynamic perspective involves questions designed to elicit hidden beliefs, conceptions of selfhood, and perception of others. Through the LM, the goal was to reveal how Monroe *mentalized* her feelings, desires, wishes, goals, and attitudes—a process that comes under the psychodynamic rubric of "reflective functioning" (Luyten et al. 2020). Mentalizing is guided by embedded mental representations, through which individuals explain their own behavior and their perceptions of the behaviors of other human beings. So, we now focus on Monroe's mentalizing process, which is revealed by how she represented herself and others and how she explained the representations.

Let us consider Monroe's letter again. This time we designed prompts (the *Questioner*), aiming to access her state of mind further:

Monroe: Just now when I looked out the hospital window where the snow had covered everything suddenly everything is kind of a muted green.
Questioner: It seems that the scenic view that you describe is very sad.
Monroe: The grass, shabby evergreen bushes—though the trees give me a little hope—the desolate bare branches promising maybe there will be spring and maybe they promise hope.

The LM then generated the following output:

Questioner: That must be very painful to have those visions and see them come true.
Monroe: My father is still alive, but I can't call him that anymore.
Questioner: I understand.
Monroe: I can't bear the tears or the pain anymore.
Questioner: I understand.

Monroe: I am going to take my life.
Questioner: I understand.
Monroe: I am going to give in.
Questioner: You don't have to do that.
Monroe: I don't have any choice.
Questioner: You can try.

In this output, there is some irrelevant and incorrect factual information ("My father is still alive"), but it does reveal the sense of despair and suicidal intention that Monroe certainly must have felt, given her subsequent suicide. In effect, the LM gives us access to a deeply hidden psychodynamic mentalizing layer, revealed by our Virtual Monroe admitting that tears have fallen from her face without her knowing why. We then explored this line of analysis further by employing Google's Natural Language API demo,[3] an automatic tool for text analysis. From this we were able to identify the dominant sentiment in Monroe's text as a negative one. So, we then used the following prompt designed to access Monroe's mentalizing process:

Questioner: Can you try and explain why did you cry?

The output generated by the LM is shown below:

Monroe: I suppose it was that sequence—they shot it so quickly. I don't
   know what it is that gives me the feeling of being alone and disconnected. I haven't been very well over the past two or three months.
   I'm not totally recovered and if I were going to take a trip—I don't
   know what the trip would be like. I've had some very real fears.

Not all the parts of the output turned out to be relevant, and those are thus dismissed. The relevant ones involve our Virtual Monroe admitting that she is alone and disconnected, that she is not "very well," and that she has some "real fears." While the real-life Monroe never explained her state of mind or even named its effects ("crying") in the original text, the LM, prompted by our question, has unraveled how she must have mentalized it, thus deepening our understanding of Monroe's inner world. Her answer to the question "Can you try and explain why did you cry?" is a reflective one, revealing that she had "very real fears."

In a later segment of her letter, Monroe relates how she burst into tears after seeing a photo of Sigmund Freud on the inside cover of a book she was reading. She interpreted the photo as revealing that Freud was a depressed and disappointed person—a conclusion she came to after having read one of Freud's letters in the book. Prompting the Virtual Monroe to explain this impression, we introduced the following question, which produced the response shown below:

Questioner: You looked at Freud's picture and burst into tears. Why did you cry? What made you so sad?
Monroe: Freud was a very disappointed man. As we all are. I was just very emotional about it. I was very upset. I was upset for a lot of reasons.

By describing Freud as a "disappointed man" in her letter, Monroe was likely projecting her own inner disappointment and pain onto him, and the Virtual Monroe rationalized this with "As we all are." In other words, the Virtual Monroe suggests that Monroe was trying to understand herself through someone else. Again, it is remarkable that the LM allowed us to enter Monroe's mind, seemingly pinpointing how she mentalized her emotional pain. Our LM was thus a very talented "psychotherapist," so to speak. We will return to the case of the actress in chapter 6. Our objective here was to show how powerful the LM can be in fleshing out hidden subtexts in a text, via a hypothetical dialogue with the text-maker. This is truly a remarkable feat, since the virtual dialogue could actually be projected onto reality as a means of understanding what Monroe tragically ended up doing.

The Joker

As a second illustrative case in point of what the LM is capable of achieving in textual analysis, again using psychodynamic theory, consider the movie *Joker* (2019), directed by Todd Phillips, which was intended on the surface to provide an origin story for the villain of Batman lore. Set in 1981, the plot follows Arthur Fleck, a failed clown and comedian who becomes mentally unbalanced and whose nihilism ignites a violent revolution against the wealthy denizens in a decaying Gotham City. Movie critics have seen the film as dealing with mental illness and its effects, constituting a kind of cautionary tale about a society whose disregard of less fortunate people is bound to produce a person like the Joker. Now, we decided to test this view on the basis of various statements made by Arthur in the movie, utilizing the LM to help us flesh out any hidden meanings in them.

We started with a key dialogue that takes place between Arthur and the social worker assigned to him. In it, the worker is clearly attempting to find out how Arthur feels about their own encounters and whether they are having any positive effect on him. The Joker (i.e., Arthur) indicates that they are useless. So, we got the LM to reconstruct the dialogue with a prompt that we assigned to a virtual social worker:

Worker: Do you feel like you want to get better?
Arthur: You know, if I don't feel better, I'm not going to live.

The AI indicates that our Virtual Arthur is experiencing negative emotions that might induce him to commit suicide ("I'm not going to live"), unless he can shed these emotions ("if I don't feel better"). We then introduced a prompt asking for an explanation, which led to the following dialogue:

Worker: Why do you think that you are not going to live?
Arthur: Because I'm crazy.
Worker: How do you know that you are crazy?
Arthur: I don't know.
Worker: No, you don't have to know.
Arthur: Well, I'm crazy.
Worker: Why do you think you are crazy?
Arthur: Because I keep getting locked up again and again.
Worker: Have you ever felt suicidal?
Arthur: I've thought about it.

As this stretch of virtual dialogue brings out, our prompt led the LM to adopt a psychodynamic approach related to Arthur's suicidal state of mind, which he confirmed. At that point, we introduced a prompt that elicited the following response by our Virtual Arthur:

Worker: Can you explain why?
Arthur: I don't have anything to live for.

This answer is truly remarkable, revealing a similar pattern of thought to that discovered in our Virtual Monroe's pattern of responses. At first blush, watching the Joker in the movie may lead us to perceive him as a psychopath only; however, as our LM discovered, this may be a misinterpretation. The reconstructed dialogue between the Joker and the social worker reveals the depth of depression and sense of meaninglessness that the Joker is experiencing, which can easily be missed in a surface reading of the film. The LM was able to flesh out the deep psychic angst that the Joker was feeling, thus explaining his aberrant behavior in the film more meaningfully. The LM thus not only carried out a remarkable psychodynamic assessment but also provided a critical stance from which to reframe the accepted interpretation of the movie and of Arthur's character as that of a psychopath. Our actual empathy for the film character can now be understood as our own unconscious sense that he is deeply disturbed (as was Monroe), with signs of a deep depression.

Summary

As the two examples discussed in this chapter saliently show, AI can indeed talk with texts, so to speak, in order to penetrate below the surface, generating virtual dialogues, on the basis of the DNN's modeling of the lexical–contextual information in the texts, and bringing out hidden meanings for us to consider. While the LM's assessment is speculative, it is highly plausible. In the case of the Monroe letter, it was able to actually "sense" her subsequent tragic act. To use José Ortega y Gasset's (1959) insight here, initially a text such as Monroe's letter is deficient, since it really does not tell the whole story; with the LM, however, we can read between its lines so as to reveal subtexts of which Monroe herself may not have been aware.

Given that the LM is trained on a huge dataset, it is obvious that it can be used constructively to flesh out delicate patterns that are hidden to the author and analyst alike. In terms of the SFP (chapter 1), it can be said that the LM has the capacity to extend the range of interpretations by locating "silent" signs standing for deep loneliness and alienation, thus resolving what Gasset (1959) called the "difficulty of reading" that any text presents. The LM has an advantage in resolving this difficulty, because it is not involved emotionally in the reconstruction process, as might be, for example, a psychotherapist or a movie critic. It is thus a powerful hermeneutic aid in the interpretive process. The prompts inputted into the LM are, of course, devised by human interpreters, who are paying selective attention to certain sections of the text. These are theoretically based prompts that are indispensable in getting the LM to enter into a virtual dialogue with the text. A playwright seeking to understand Monroe for, say, a play about her could use the AI profitably to make her characterization more realistic and emotionally powerful. Analogously, a psychotherapist who is treating a patient exhibiting the same kinds of self-representations as those discovered by the LM with respect to Monroe could also profitably use the AI method to gain insights into the kind of therapy required.

Notes

1 The letter can be found at www.thevintagenews.com/2016/04/19/the-sad-letter-that-marylin-monroe-sent-to-her-psychiatrist
2 https://6b.eleuther.ai. The reader can consult this open demo of LM at this website.
3 See https://cloud.google.com/natural-language#section-2

References

Borges, J. L. [1941] (1999). *Garden of Forking Paths*. New York: Penguin.
Gasset, J. O. y (1959). The Difficulty of Reading. *Diogenes* 7: 1–17.

Holquist, M. (1990). *Dialogism*. London: Routledge.

Licklider, J. C. R. (1960). Man-Computer Symbiosis. *IRE Transactions on Human Factors in Electronics* HFE-1: 4–11.

Lingiardi, V. and McWilliams, N. (eds.) (2017). *Psychodynamic Diagnostic Manual: PDM-2*. New York: Guilford Press.

Lingiardi, V., McWilliams, N., Bornstein, R. F., Gazzillo, F., and Gordon, R. M. (2015). The Psychodynamic Diagnostic Manual Version 2 (PDM-2): Assessing Patients for Improved Clinical Practice and Research. *Psychoanalytic Psychology* 32(1): 94–115.

Luyten, P., Campbell, C., Allison, E., and Fonagy, P. (2020). The Mentalizing Approach to Psychopathology: State of the Art and Future Directions. *Annual Review of Clinical Psychology* 16: 297–325.

Petitmengin, C., Remillieux, A., and Valenzuela-Moguillansky, C. (2019). Discovering the Structures of Lived Experience. *Phenomenology and the Cognitive Sciences* 18(4): 691–730.

5 Bart Simpson
The Rebellious Mind

Bart Simpson

The animated sitcom *The Simpsons*, created by cartoonist Matt Groening, is one of the longest-running programs on American television, starting in 1987 as a weekly feature on *The Tracey Ullman Show* and then debuting as a separate program in 1989. The sitcom is a satire of bourgeois middle-class American life, as well as a parody of aspects of contemporary society and its pretentions. The question of what lies below the textual surface of the sitcom will be addressed in this chapter, using psychologically based prompting strategies to get the LM to identify why audiences have enjoyed the program for such a long period of time. Our main focus is the character of Bart Simpson, aiming to expose his rebellious personality as a plausible reason why he has remained so popular among television audiences, perhaps reflecting an instinctive rebellious attitude within American society toward authority figures. Bart challenges authority at the same time that he cleverly avoids punishment. Our Virtual Bart can provide insights into his rebellious attitudes, which we can then utilize to gain a perspective on the role of the rebellious spirit in American culture.

Bart's name is a clue to his character—it is an anagram of the word *brat*. At ten years of age, he is the oldest child and only son of Homer and Marge, and brother to Lisa and Maggie. In virtually all the episodes of the sitcom, Bart's disrespect for authority is a central theme. This comes out through his gags, his prank calls, and his catchphrases, such as "Eat my shorts," "Don't have a cow, man," and "I'm Bart Simpson. Who the hell are you?" Significantly, during the opening seasons, Bart became the most popular character on the show, as "Bartmania" ensued, spawning related merchandise ironically symbolizing his rebellious attitude and pride at underachieving, which actually caused many parents and educators to cast Bart as a bad role model for children—a view that never caught on broadly.

DOI: 10.4324/9781003331407-5

The Vandalizing Episode of Season One

Psychoanalysis has at times been in a close partnership with semiotics because, as Sigmund Freud himself claimed, the former (like the latter) is an interpretive art. In psychoanalytic theory, symbols are critical tokens because they often disguise hidden wishes and desires. Freud (1901: 286) put it as follows:

> Symbolism is not peculiar to dreams, but is characteristic of unconscious ideation, in particular, among people, and is to be found in folklore, and in popular myths, legends, linguistic idioms, proverbial wisdom and current jokes, to a more complete extent than in dreams.

The key notion in the Freudian approach is that of the "unconscious" (Freud 1963: 235–236), a deep layer of the psyche that is usually inaccessible to reflective awareness. The LM can actually be envisioned as a Freudian AI (so to speak), given its ability to penetrate unconscious meanings hidden in the lexico-semantic structures used to create texts, as we saw in the previous chapter.

A key aspect of the unconscious mind is that it seeks gratification but cannot express it openly because it must submit to the demands of society—demands that might cause considerable mental anguish. So, a fictional representation such as *The Simpsons* is a textual form that allows for gratification and pleasure to be expressed safely via the representation itself, which Freud called the "pleasure principle." Without binding ourselves to the Freudian perspective outright, there is little doubt that his principle can be enlisted as a hypothetical framework for explaining the appeal of *The Simpsons*.

In an essay titled "Psychopathic Characters on the Stage," Freud (1942) explicitly explained that the function of drama is to allow the repressed need for pleasure and enjoyment to be expressed. The stage involves a suspension of disbelief whereby we can project ourselves into an imaginary world in order to understand ourselves, at the same time that we are consciously aware that we are in a made-up world. When we observe a man-eating shark in the movie *Jaws* (1975), for example, we are catapulted psychologically into the fearful situation via the imagination, whereby we experience a chilling thrill, as if we were actually in a real situation, at the same time that we are perfectly aware that we are inside an illusion and thus not physically in danger. To recall Mikhail Bakhtin's (2021) two orders (chapter 1), we can locate an art form, such as drama, at the intersection between real-life experience and the representation of that experience, which produces an aesthetic effect (thrill, joy, fear, etc.). Between art and life there is no clear boundary but the boundary marking the "potential space" (Winnicott 1968) of play.

As Freud suggested, the representation of *struggle* and *suffering* is common in the theater—both are impulses for enacting rebellion against metaphysical forces such as destiny. As he observed, the spectator does not actually engage in the struggle or suffering displayed by the fictitious characters but can vicariously participate in them, and thus become engaged by emotional proxy in the characters' actions, such as rebellion against authority figures, without paying the price that a rebel pays in real life. It is this surrogate engagement via the dramatic representation that is, arguably, the source of pleasure elicited by *The Simpsons*, which provides a fictional format for identifying with Bart as a rebel, without paying any price for the rebelliousness. Bart is the epitome of the rebellious child, continuously and fearlessly challenging authority figures and social norms. A crowd-sourced rating of Bart's personality[1] has actually identified the traits of *mischievous* (not well behaved) and *rebellious* (not obedient) as his two most conspicuous personality traits. By talking with a Virtual Bart, we may come to a deeper understanding of his character and gain insights into the reasons behind Bart's appeal to large audiences.

We start our analysis with the "vandalizing" episode from the first season.[2] The episode takes place in school, where Bart is caught by the principal—Principal Skinner—vandalizing school property. Below is the relevant dialogue—between Bart, Skinner, Martin (Bart's classmate), and Milhouse (Bart's best friend):

Skinner: No chewing gum on school grounds. Throw it in the trashcan.
Martin: One of my fellow students is vandalizing school property, Principal Skinner.
Skinner: Really? Where?
Martin: See over there, sir?
Milhouse: Bart, look out! Here comes Skinner.
Bart: Yikes!
Skinner: The student who did this is in deep trouble.
…
Skinner: Simpson, we're going to have a serious talk.
Bart: Same time, same place?
Skinner: Correct. After school, in my office.
All: Ooh!

Principal Skinner is clearly an authority figure, who will likely mete out some punishment to Bart for vandalizing the school's property; this perception comes from an unconscious understanding that any breach of social norms will entail a pain-inducing response from the authorities. It is based, in other words, on our sense that any act of rebellion involves suffering and struggle. This is perhaps why we empathize with Bart and, indirectly, gain a form of satisfaction for our own ersatz (hidden) rebellion. Through the episode, we might even recall the pain and fear of being summoned to the principal's office after doing something illicit or prohibited during our own school years. But, unlike Bart, we do not have to face any consequences—just literally sit back and observe the situation unfold. It is no coincidence that the principal is named Skinner, alluding to the famous (or infamous for some) behavioral psychologist and his negative conditioning experiments, which involved punishments.

Given the symbolic nature of the human mind and the way it generalizes from specific instances (Neuman 2020), Principal Skinner is perceived not just as a specific individual but as a symbolic "father figure," who dispenses punishments for violations of norms and for disruptive behaviors. This is the contextual information that must be inputted into the LM, since it underlies the anxiety produced by the episode, whereby we expect Bart to be punished by such a figure for violating the social order and challenging authority. This is based on: (a) Milhouse's warning ("Bart, look out!"); (b) the principal's own warning ("The student who did this is in deep trouble"); (c) Martin's imputation that Bart is a vandalizer ("One of my fellow students is vandalizing school property"); (d) Skinner's admonition that he and Bart must have a "serious talk;" and (e) the reaction of the students on the scene ("Ooh!"), which can imply pain or ironic commentary. As Freud suggested, suffering is inherent in all genres of drama, either explicitly or by implication, and, given Bart's violation of the social norms and the reactions it elicited, our expectation is that he will endure some form of suffering for his vandalism. Significantly, Bart, as a true rebel, does not seem concerned at all about any imminent disciplining. To grasp what lies below the surface of the episode, we will use the LM to generate a conversation with a Virtual Bart.

Character Analysis: Part I

The first step in the dialogical reconstruction is to devise a prompt designed to invite Bart to "reflect" on his behavior. "Reflective functioning" or "mentalizing" (Luyten et al. 2020) is the capacity to understand oneself and others in terms of embedded mental representations. As portrayed in the sitcom, Bart appears to be quite limited in the ability to mentalize his inner thoughts, given his young age and his character, which is oriented toward external, rather than internal, expressivity. This suggests that Bart may be an extravert who manifests signs of attention deficit disorder. Consequently, Bart is incapable of grasping his inner mental states overtly, so as to be able to successfully navigate the social world (Anis et al. 2020). By prompting our Virtual Bart to actually reflect upon his actions, we may have a better understanding of the covert part of his character and inner states. The LM might then provide us with a "potential space" (Winnicott 1968) in which reality and a representation of reality can converge as we "play" with the text in our imagination. The first question below was our initial prompt. This then allowed the LM to construct a relevant dialogue with the Virtual Bart:

Questioner: Bart, why did you vandalize the school's property?
Bart: To make a point.
Questioner: What is the point in vandalizing school property?
Bart: To be a criminal.
Questioner: Do you see yourself as a criminal?
Bart: No.
Questioner: It doesn't make sense. You said that you vandalized school property to be a criminal. However, you denied that you are a criminal.

The second prompt ("Do you see yourself as a criminal?") is in line with the psychodynamic approach, aiming to penetrate Bart's beliefs about his own sense of self. The comment that "It doesn't make sense" is based on the Psychodiagnostics Chart–2 (Gordon and Borenstein 2018), which aims to unravel the subject's sense of personal identity and the ability to view oneself in complex, stable, and accurate ways. Bart's (virtual) answer, "To be a criminal," to the clarification question, "What is the point in vandalizing school property?" is a non sequitur and inconsistent with his subsequent response that he does not consider himself to be a criminal. So, after his incoherence is challenged ("It doesn't make sense"), the Virtual Bart answers as follows:

Bart: I wasn't a criminal. I was an anarchist.

This is an unexpected answer—that is, the Virtual Bart, who previously described himself as a "criminal," unexpectedly corrects his self-description to "anarchist." So, what does this imply? We continue by asking the following prompt, to which the Virtual Bart answers as shown:

Questioner: What's the difference between a criminal and an anarchist?
Bart: An anarchist is against the system.

This again is a truly remarkable response. Bart, an elementary school student, who has just vandalized school property, should logically be labeled as a juvenile "criminal," as he initially asserts, subject to punishment by an authority figure. Identifying with criminals is vastly different than identifying with rebels. We react fearfully to the former but with empathy to the latter. The Virtual Bart's self-description as an "anarchist against the system" is a perfect description of what a rebel is essentially all about. It is through the reconstructive dialogical process—talking with the text through theoretically guided mediation—that the LM is able to "diagnose" Bart as an anarchist against the system. To put it differently, the LM was in no way directed to reach this diagnosis—it came about through a deep neural network analysis, involving the extraction of linguistic–contextual patterns that the prompt put in motion. The result is a deepening of our understanding of Bart on the basis of a single episode.

We then used further prompting to explore the minutiae of Bart's personality. The following dialogue is the result of prompting tailored from what is written about Bart on Wikipedia (2022):

Questioner: Hi Bart.
Bart: Hi.
Questioner: To know you better, I would like you to introduce yourself.
Bart: What do you mean?
Questioner: For example, how old are you, who is your family, things that you like to do and so on.
Bart: OK. I'm ten years old. My father is Homer, and my mother is Marge. I have two sisters, Lisa and Maggie.
Questioner: Nice. And where do you live?
Bart: In Springfield.
Questioner: So you are currently in school?
Bart: Yes, I'm a 4th grade student at Springfield Elementary School.
Questioner: So you are a student and what do you like to do in your free time?
Bart: I like skateboarding, watching TV, reading comic books (especially *Radioactive Man*), and playing video games.
Questioner: Interesting. What is your favorite TV show?
Bart: The *Krusty the Clown Show*, which includes *The Itchy & Scratchy Show*.

At this point, we used this constructed dialogue as a subsequent input, returning to the vandalizing episode and repeating the same question that we had previously asked. The LM then generated the dialogue below:

Questioner: Bart, why did you vandalize the school's property?

Output

Bart: I don't know. I just like to do things that nobody else does.
Questioner: What? You mean you just like to do things for fun?
Bart: Yeah, I like to skateboard, watch TV, read comic books, and play video games.
Questioner: And what does this mean for your education?
Bart: It means I'm way behind in my classes.

Bart's first response suggests that he is a non-reflective person, since he cannot explain his behavior. Paradoxically, he actually then indicates that he likes to do things that nobody else does, which is an unconscious form of self-assessment. The LM then generates a correct guess, namely that Bart is a *low achiever*. Indeed, Bart is presented in the sitcom as such. The guess was made possible simply by contextualizing the dialogue, incorporating background knowledge and the description of a specific event, which tells us something about Bart that is not explicit in any prompt. The LM thus accurately predicted that an elementary school student who likes to skateboard and who is involved in vandalizing school property is a low achiever—a verity of real life.

Character Analysis: Part II

To deepen our understanding of Bart's character, we hypothesized that his act of vandalism might be the expression of a sensation-seeking or impulsive urge, as Freud himself might have suggested. Recall that our Virtual Bart perceives himself as an "anarchist," a term with political–ideological connotations in the neural network; however, the source of this self-description clearly has nothing to do with politics, but rather with a hunch that it reveals an impulsive sensation-seeking personality, which Bart justifies or masks in ideological terms. It was this context that led us to devise a relevant prompt that generates a dialogue based on questions focusing on the established psychological assessments of personality, which emerge from each response (indicated in square brackets):

Questioner: It seems that you are a joyful child.
Bart: Yes, I have a lot of fun, I amuse my friends and laugh a lot. [Extravert]
Questioner: So, you are a friendly boy too.
Bart: Sure. I make friends easy and love to party with them. [Extravert]
Questioner: And if you like skateboarding then it seems that you like adventures too.

Bart: Sure! I seek adventures and danger, love action and to act wild and crazy. [Sensation-seeking]
Questioner: Are you afraid of the danger?
Bart: No! I love danger! [Sensation-seeking]
Questioner: But, doesn't it get you into trouble?
Bart: Well sure.
Questioner: Can you explain?
Bart: Sometimes I react without thinking about it. [Impulsive]
Questioner: It may get you into trouble.
Bart: Yes, I know but I don't care. [Impulsive]
Questioner: Really?
Bart: Sure. I love trouble. [Low agreeableness, rebellious]
Questioner: What kind of trouble?
Bart: I have a sharp tongue and don't mind insulting people and cutting them to pieces. [Low agreeableness, rebellious]
Questioner: So, you enjoy clashing with other people?
Bart: I do. You see, I lose interest very quickly and get bored. [Sensation-seeking]
Questioner: And fighting with others is a way of finding interest?
Bart: Sure, it's fun.

Clearly, this artificial dialogue that we have created represents some key traits that are associated with a rebellious personality—sensation-seeking, low agreeableness, impulsivity, and extraversion. We use it as a context for fine tuning the LM and then introduce a prompt asking the Virtual Bart what he thought about Principal Skinner. This was also based on the psychodynamic approach, aiming to decode Bart's beliefs about authority figures. We contextualized the input by providing the LM with some guidelines as to how to filter Bart's hypothetical personality. Below is the prompt followed by the virtual dialogue:

Questioner: What do you think about Principal Skinner?

Output

Bart: I hate him.
Questioner: Why?
Bart: Because he's the principal.
Questioner: Do you mean Principal Skinner as an authority figure?
Bart: No. I mean Principal Skinner as Principal Skinner.
Questioner: Oh. He's a very nice man.
Bart: No, he isn't.

Questioner: Why not?
Bart: He's too strict.
Questioner: Really?
Bart: Yes. He takes away the games of the kids and all the stuff.

Notice that the word "authority" did not appear in the prompt; nonetheless, the LM generated the hypothesis that Bart "hates" Principal Skinner because he is too strict (as an authority figure is expected to be). The Virtual Bart thus exposes an emotion (hate) that did not appear in the episode, evoked by the principal's "strict" behavior, against which Bart (as a rebel) inveighs, since it imposes limits on his sensation-seeking activities. We then used this dialogue as new input, repeating the relevant question and getting the following dialogue as output:

Questioner: Bart, why did you vandalize the school's property?

Output

Bart: I was bored and thought it'd be fun to vandalize school property.
Questioner: But you shouldn't.
Bart: Why not?
Questioner: Because you are a child and children have to respect authority.
Bart: You sound like my parents.
Questioner: How do I sound like your parents?
Bart: You speak a lot about authority and all that.
Questioner: Yes. I'm an authority figure myself.
Bart: Really?
Questioner: Yes.

This final part of the dialogue summarizes what a non-ideological rebel—someone who possesses a deep aversion to authority of any kind—is all about. The *Questioner* insists on getting an answer as to why Bart vandalized school property, to which Bart answers that the reason was boredom, and, when egged on to accept the legitimacy of authority figures such as parents and even the *Questioner*, our Virtual Bart becomes perplexed, as is expected of someone who is actually rebellious, seeing in their actions a justification for going against authority. Is it this aspect of Bart's character that is so appealing? The answer seems to be yes, given that Bart Simpson remains to this day the most beloved *Simpsons* character. Remarkably, we achieved this interpretation on the basis of a virtual dialogue based on a single episode, generated by our AI dialoguing with the text.

Summary

In this chapter, the LM was used as a "mediator," which is the idea (in cultural psychology) of "acting with mediational means" (Wertsch 1995). As Alex Gillespie and Tania Zittoun (2010: 45) remark, "Tools, according to Vygotsky, mediate our relation to the physical world, and signs mediate our relation to our own or other minds." Our mediator was the LM, which utilized contextual information together with prompts to unravel Bart's character and personality. It mediated our relation with the character within an in-between space (fictive reality and imagination), which allowed the AI to produce a personality profile of a rebel who is a thrill-seeker and averse to authority figures. This might be the real reason why the Bart Simpson character is so broadly appealing. Bart is not perceived as a "criminal" but as a true American rebel.

In a fundamental way, Bart is a symbol of the American rebel, who has played a real role in the history of America. The AI updated the explanation of why America is still fascinated with this iconic–heroic sign, which started with the colonists of the Thirteen Colonies, who rejected British rule. Bart is not a rebel in the political sense, but a "rebel without a (political) cause," so to speak. He emblemizes an unconscious rebellious instinct in American groupthink, which, as writer Norman Mailer (1957: 276) has aptly observed, is part of a "hip" image that people seemingly aspire to embody.

We also discovered another hidden aspect of Bart's character through the AI—namely that his actions are designed to combat boredom ("I lose interest very quickly and get bored"). Given that there is no documentary evidence (writings) of boredom until the nineteenth century, where it is discussed perhaps for the first time in Charles Dickens' novel *Bleak House*, the relevant question is: Would a character such as Bart Simpson be conceivable in any era other than the contemporary one? Young rebels see themselves as the antidote to boredom. It is no coincidence therefore that Bart has become such a powerful symbol of ersatz rebellion—perhaps a rebellion against the boredom of modern-day society.

Notes

1 See https://openpsychometrics.org/tests/characters/stats/S/2
2 See www.kaggle.com/prashant111/the-simpsons-dataset

References

Anis, L., Perez, G., Benzies, K. M., Ewashen, C., Hart, M., and Letourneau, N. (2020). Convergent Validity of Three Measures of Reflective Function: Parent

Development Interview, Parental Reflective Function Questionnaire, and Reflective Function Questionnaire. *Frontiers in Psychology* 16. https://doi.org /10.3389/fpsyg.2020.574719.

Freud, S. (1901). *The Interpretation of Dreams*. New York: Avon.

Freud, S. (1942). Psychopathic Characters on the Stage. *Psychoanalytic Quarterly* 11(4): 459–464.

Freud, S. (1963). *Civilization and Its Discontents*. London: Hogarth.

Gillespie, A. and Zittoun, T. (2010). Using Resources: Conceptualizing the Mediation and Reflective Use of Tools and Signs. *Culture and Psychology* 16(1): 37–62.

Gordon, R. M. and Bornstein, R. F. (2018). Construct Validity of the Psychodiagnostic Chart: A Transdiagnostic Measure of Personality Organization, Personality Syndromes, Mental Functioning, and Symptomatology. *Psychoanalytic Psychology* 35(2): 280–288.

Luyten, P., Campbell, C., Allison, E., and Fonagy, P. (2020). The Mentalizing Approach to Psychopathology: State of the Art and Future Directions. *Annual Review of Clinical Psychology* 16: 297–325.

Mailer, N. (1957). Superficial Reflections on the Hipster. *Dissent*. https://www .dissentmagazine.org/online_articles/the-white-negro-fall-1957.

Neuman, Y. (2020). *Conceptual Mathematics and Literature: Toward a Deep Reading of Texts and Minds*. Leiden: Brill.

Wertsch, J. V. (1995). The Need for Action in Sociocultural Research. In: J. V. Wertsch, P. Del Rio, and A. Alvarez (eds.), *Sociocultural Studies of Mind*, 56–74. Cambridge: Cambridge University Press.

Wikipedia (2022). Bart Simpson. https://en.wikipedia.org/wiki/Bart_Simpson.

Winnicott, D. W. (1968). Playing: Its Theoretical Status in the Clinical Situation. *International Journal of Psycho-Analysis* 49: 591–599.

6 Marilyn Monroe
Are Diamonds Really a Girl's Best Friend?

Monroe's Screen Persona and Her True Self

In chapter 4, we put forth a psychological assessment of Marilyn Monroe's depressive state on the basis of a letter she wrote while hospitalized, which the LM was able to turn into a virtual dialogical text in which suicidal thoughts were fleshed out of the Virtual Monroe's reconstructed words. It is remarkable that the LM was able to do this, given the fact that Monroe tragically ended her life shortly after that letter.

In this chapter, we go a little deeper into analyzing the painful emotional gap that emerged between Monroe's screen persona and her real "true" self. Using the same approach as described previously, we enlist Monroe's own autobiography as the input text from which the LM will be able to generate its dialogue. The specific psychological theory used for our prompts is that of attachment theory (Bowlby 1953, 1971), which claims that young children need to develop a loving relationship with at least one primary caregiver in order for them to develop a healthy personality in social and emotional terms. By reconstructing our Virtual Monroe, we seek to decode the source of her anxiety and the sad consequences that it brought about. The mediation AI in this case turned out to be not only a simple tool for augmenting the human interpretation of Monroe's life, but a means to grasp the nature of the emotional gap between Monroe's true and artificially constructed selves, and thus a means to understand why "diamonds are really not a girl's best friend." As is widely known, the song "Diamonds Are a Girl's Best Friend" was introduced by Carol Channing in the original Broadway production of *Gentlemen Prefer Blondes* (1949). But it is mainly associated with Monroe in the 1953 film version of the musical. In the movie, Monroe's character, Lorelei Lee, performs the song, which is about exploiting men, in a cabaret, even though her aspirations are just the opposite of those of a gold-digger. Monroe's rendition of the song and the pink dress she wore have become iconic symbols, inspiring subsequent homages by pop singers.

DOI: 10.4324/9781003331407-6

As mentioned in chapter 4, Monroe was one of Hollywood's most famous stars, portrayed as a "sex symbol" who helped ensconce the "blonde bombshell" stereotype in popular culture. This was her screen persona—a sexually available but artificial person (Churchwell 2005). However, as we learned from the LM-mediated interpretation, her real personality was vastly different. The gap between the two is one possible reason for her depressive state of mind, which ultimately led to her tragic end. Our aim in this chapter is to "talk" with Monroe by adopting attachment theory to prompt the dialogue with her virtual persona. Access to her background was made possible by her autobiographical book and personal testimonies (Monroe and Hecht 2006, Monroe 2010).

Attachment Theory

As explained by Jeremy Holmes (2017), attachment theory involves the study and understanding of the need for "interpersonally mediated security." Its relevance to our specific case in point is obvious. Young and vulnerable children, like Monroe apparently was, experience deep insecurity that might have far-reaching consequences. The "attachment" between children and caregivers is seen as crucial for both physical survival and psychological well-being. If the bond is not formed, then its lack is likely to have negative consequences for the child's subsequent experience of adulthood. The pattern of secured attachment, or lack thereof, is formed during childhood on the basis of the types of interactions the child experiences with caregivers, the child's own character and predisposition, and even the specific external situation that influences their rearing. In catastrophic situations such as wartime, where children suffer from hunger, attachment is not always possible in the same way as it is in a peaceful rearing environment.

There are various attachment patterns. A central one is called the "secure base," where a child trusts their own inner strength in order to secure a sense of safety from danger and a capacity to explore their inner and outer worlds freely. This is not equivalent to the satisfaction of basic needs. It emerges through meaningful interactions with others in the rearing environment who love the child and teach them how to cope with stress and anxiety (directly or indirectly), allowing the child to react resiliently to different kinds of situations. As such, the child develops a positive inner representation of how emotional security is realized. According to current attachment theory, mental resilience correlates with the functional and adaptive nature of such representations. A secure and resilient person may overcome a stressful situation simply by approaching it mentally in terms of how it is represented in their mind (from previous experiences). For example, insecure children may blame themselves for the painful divorce of their parents, suffering depression as a consequence of this belief; in contrast, a secure child may still experience pain from a divorce, but will frame it differently in a contextualized way, so as to grasp the situation as occurring from outside rather than from inside so as to ease the pain. The secure child may also perceive the situation historically, focusing on the good years spent together with the parents and accepting that things change, and thus that a new path should be pursued.

In the case of an insecure upbringing, which was the case with Monroe, three general emotional personality types tend to develop, as identified by the relevant research studies:

1. The *anxious* insecure individual, who fears abandonment and who thus experiences depression and low self-esteem. The individual's stressful experiences are expressed through self-blame.
2. The *avoidant* individual, who is emotionally detached in relationships, lacking the ability to form intimate bonds. Having experienced stress, individuals who fall into this category typically feel that they are simply "not there," coping with stress by emotionally detaching themselves from any negative or menacing experience.
3. The *disorganized* individual, who feels deeply insecure and fearful of establishing meaningful relationships. The individual attempts to establish attachments but is incapable of doing so—hence the disorganized (inconsistent) behavior varying between avoidance and irrational clinging that is typical among such individuals. This is the most problematic of all attachment disorders, and it is associated with the borderline personality disorder.

It is significant to stress again that modern attachment theories emphasize the importance of mental *representation* (Holmes 2010, 2017)—whereby attachment relationships with others become internal representations formed in childhood but in a deeper sense; it is the representation of relations, whether valid or not, which is the most important thing, rather than the experience itself.

To cite Holmes (2010: 49), the way an individual talks about themselves or the external world is the key to decoding the type of attachment image that the individual has, including if the person is insecure in an anxious, avoidant, or disorganized way, and thus how the individual processes emotions and represents security, trust, intimacy, and anxiety. Exposing these representations through AI mediation might help to shed light specifically on how an individual understands themselves and the world. Thus, the contextualized information (such as childhood rearing) that shapes the inner representation is key to grasping the nature of Monroe's depressive state, given that her experience of childhood included an unknown father, a mother who suffered from a mental breakdown herself, growing up in an orphanage and foster families, and being the victim of sexual abuse. Monroe can be characterized, initially, as having an anxious disorganized personality. Compounding this later in life was an early marriage that ended in divorce. To grasp her inner angst, we will utilize, as mentioned, Monroe's autobiography, submitting it to the LM for analysis, via a psychological interview based on prompts derived from attachment theory.

Monroe's Virtual Interview

From background sources (including online ones such as the Wikipedia entry dealing with Monroe), we learn that Monroe—whose birth name was Norma Jeane Mortenson and who was later baptized as Norma Jeane Baker—spent much of her childhood in foster care and in an orphanage, because she was abandoned by her father and because her mother, being mentally ill, could not raise her. A particularly important aspect of her upbringing was that a family friend and her husband took care of her for a few years. The couple was deeply religious and followed fundamentalist doctrine, inhibiting Monroe from experiencing a typical upbringing, such as by going to the movies. At seven years old, Monroe returned to a life in foster homes, where she endured sexual abuse. She dropped out of high school at 15. One year later, in 1942, Monroe sought a way out of her negative emotional quagmire through an early marriage to merchant marine Jimmy Dougherty.

Monroe never knew who her real father was. She once even thought that actor Clark Gable was her father—a story repeated by various sources. However, there is no evidence that this is true in any way. As an adult, Monroe claimed that one of her earliest traumatic memories was of her mother trying to smother her in her crib with a pillow. During her short lifetime, Monroe married and divorced three different men: Dougherty (above), New York Yankees baseball star Joe DiMaggio, and playwright Arthur Miller, whom she married in 1956. From the outset, the marriage to Miller was troubled, with Monroe abusing alcohol and prescription drugs, which had a severe impact on her mental stability. She became even more depressed when she suffered a miscarriage. After a second miscarriage, she became increasingly dependent on alcohol and pills for comfort. Probably to save the marriage, Miller wrote a screenplay called *The Misfits* (1961), giving Monroe a leading role. However, the couple's relationship continued deteriorating during the production of the film. The ensuing divorce was the beginning of the end for Monroe. All three of her marriages had failed, and she was unable to give birth to the child she craved. She died in 1962 of a barbiturate overdose at her home in Los Angeles. The death was deemed to be a probable suicide, but this is still contested by some forensic scientists and historians. Our textual interaction with Monroe in chapter 4, however, seems to have identified suicide as the most likely manner of death.

Our virtual psychological interview here is based on the opening chapter of Monroe's autobiography (Monroe and Hecht 2006), as well as relevant information on her early life from various sources. Our prompts were adapted from the Adult Attachment Interview (George, Kaplan, and Main 1987), and our interview is divided into two parts: (a) one aiming to establish Monroe's memories of her childhood and (b) her memories of her own mentally ill mother.

Monroe's Childhood Memories

This part of the interview was designed to assess the impact of Monroe's negative childhood experiences. Our *Questioner* in this case is named the *Psychotherapist*, and the answers provided by Monroe are formed based on her biography. We then used the interview as a context for prompting the LM further. Here are three examples that the LM produced:

Example 1

Psychotherapist: Hi Marilyn. I will interview you about your childhood experiences and how they may have shaped you as an adult. My questions will be about your early relationships with your family and so on. Firstly, let's get some family background information, such as where you were born, what your family did for a living, and whether your family moved around often.

Monroe: OK. I was born as Norma Jeane Mortenson on June 1, 1926, at the Los Angeles County Hospital in Los Angeles, California. My mother was from a poor Midwestern family. At the age of 15 ... [text has been omitted for brevity]

Psychotherapist: Marilyn, I would like you to try to describe your relationships with your family.

Monroe: Well, you must understand that I thought the people I lived with were my real parents. Only later, I found that they were not my real parents.

Example 2

Psychotherapist: Can you describe your foster parents?

Monroe: They weren't bad. They were just poor and didn't have much to give even to their own children.

Example 3

Psychotherapist: How did you feel living with your foster family?
Monroe: It was a place where I felt like a servant.

As the first chapter of Monroe's autobiography relates, she lived in uncaring situations that made optimal attachment impossible, producing a sense of anxiety within her and making her feel like a servant. As an abandoned child living in the homes of strangers or in an orphanage, Monroe had no real parents, a situation leading to a life hiding family secrets (Orgad 2014, 2015), which she exposed and whose consequences were painful. She asserts that her stepfather was the only one who ever paid any attention to her, but Monroe nonetheless perceives herself as practically invisible in the relationship. Her recollection of her real mother is that of a troubled person unable to take care of her and who actually frightens her. She also invents the persona of her missing father through a fantasy, associating him with Clark Gable on the basis of the physical similarity she perceives between a photo of her father and a photo of the famous actor. This fantasy may be the source of her decision to become an actress, in search of a comforting father figure who looks like Gable. The only other "loving figure" in her story is her dog, which is tragically killed before her own eyes.

In sum, the relevance of the opening chapter of Monroe's autobiography can be summarized in terms of several emotional sources of her deep anxiety: (a) discovering that her foster family was not her real family, (b) dealing with the fact that her mother was mentally ill, and (c) witnessing her loving dog being beaten to death in front of her eyes. In none of these situations do we find a single human figure who helps the young child cope with fear, suffering, and insecurity. Monroe's childhood clearly did not unfold in a positive rearing context, which is normally required to develop an emotionally secure base. This is further evidence in support of our assessment of the depressive pattern evident in Monroe's letter to her psychiatrist (chapter 4).

One way to grasp the influence of Monroe's childhood on her state of mind is to enlist the concept of "episodic memory"—the recollection of personal experiences associated with particular situations and events. Using a different demo[1] for our LM, we can now turn our attention to Monroe's episodic recollections of being frightened by her mother's abnormal behavior, asking our Virtual Monroe to recall the *particular* situations in which she felt frightened by her mother, so as to get access to her inner representation of the insecure attachment she had within her:

Psychotherapist: Marilyn, can you describe a specific situation where your mother frightened you?

Output

Monroe: One day I was alone in her room and she came in and asked me to sit with her. She didn't answer my question and then she started to cry. She looked at me, stared at me and then asked me what I thought was wrong with her. I didn't know what to say and she told me to be quiet.

Psychotherapist: Did she say anything else to you about her problems?

Monroe: She said she had nothing and that her husband and brother died. She said her husband drank too much and her brother wanted to be a doctor and did not like her husband.

***

Psychotherapist: Marilyn, can you describe a specific experience where your mother frightened you?

Output

Monroe: I was frightened because my mother looked at me with cold eyes and gave no sign of love or affection.

Psychotherapist: What did you think of your mother?

Monroe: I hated her.

Psychotherapist: Why?

Monroe: Because she had no feelings for me.

***

Psychotherapist: Marilyn, can you describe a specific event where your mother frightened you?

Output

Monroe: I remember when she asked me, "Who is my real mother?"

Psychotherapist: Marilyn, did you ever feel angry at your mother for taking you away?

Monroe: I was frightened when she asked me who is my mother.

Psychotherapist: Have you ever felt you are an unwanted child?

Monroe: I have.

Psychotherapist: Can you tell me why you feel like you're an unwanted child?

Monroe: I don't remember feeling loved or wanted.

While our Virtual Monroe clearly did not experience the negative feelings that the real Monroe surely did, through her, we are able to reconstruct the relevant situations that match the real Monroe's autobiographical description. Moreover, the Virtual Monroe and the Virtual Psychotherapist unravel episodic memories that do not explicitly appear in the autobiography, such as Monroe's anger toward and hatred of her mother. In describing her difficult childhood autobiographically, she never revealed these strong feelings. Providing the LM with the relevant prompting context, the virtual dialogue, on the other hand, fleshes them out, allowing us to connect them to the experience of being an "unwanted child" who never felt "loved or wanted." In this way, the LM bridges some important gaps in the original autobiography (at least in principle, if not in actuality). The process of recreating Monroe's childhood memories with the machine is an inferential one, with the output constituting no more than a hypothesis. But it is a highly plausible one, again, given the fact that the real Monroe actually experienced a painful childhood and lacked a secure emotional base, in sharp contrast with her screen persona as a secure character in total control—a contrast that can be discussed using D. W. Winnicott's (1960) concept of false self. The "false self" of Monroe (Monroe's screen persona) is thus a defensive strategy—a surrogate sense of identity. If Monroe had been given the opportunity to procure a secure base during childhood, then her screen persona could have been different. The latter took over her false sense of self, remaining in sharp contrast with her real self below the façade.

Memories of Her Mother

Monroe's memories of her mother appear to have been critical in how she came to understand herself and the world, as well as the kind of attachment pattern she developed with others (such as her husbands) as a consequence, which was to affect the rest of her life. Clearly, as the LM detected (above), this is the critical aspect in unraveling the source of Monroe's own depression. So, to clarify what kind of attachment pattern Monroe had with her mother, we used the LM to ask relevant questions about it:

Psychotherapist: Marilyn, did you ever feel hungry?

Output

Monroe: Yes. My foster parents were very poor and unable to feed me even though I was hungry.
***
Psychotherapist: Marilyn, did you feel that someone was protecting you?

Output

Monroe: No.
***

Psychotherapist: Marilyn, did you feel that your mother was protecting you?

Output

Monroe: I don't think so. I believe she was too busy taking care of herself. She didn't have time to care for me. I felt that no one was there to protect me.
***

Psychotherapist: Marilyn, did you feel that your mother loved you?

Output

Monroe: I was happy when I was with her, but I was frightened at the same time.
***

Psychotherapist: Marilyn, did you feel that anyone loved you?

Output

Monroe: I was too young to feel love.
***

Psychotherapist: Marilyn, did you feel that you could trust someone?

Output

Monroe: I didn't know what trust was.
***

Psychotherapist: Marilyn, did you feel that you could trust your mother?

Output

Monroe: I felt I couldn't trust my mother, especially when she told me that I was a bastard. I was about ten years old.
***

Psychotherapist: Marilyn, did you feel that someone could comfort you?

Output

Monroe: I would cry and cry in my room and I never felt comforted.
***
Psychotherapist: Marilyn, did you feel that your mother could comfort you?

Output

Monroe: I didn't feel that. I knew that her illness had made her very sick and tired. She was pale and her hair was very gray. She cried a lot and hardly spoke to me.

Answering our questions through the mediation of the LM and the context that we provided through Monroe's autobiographical interview, the Virtual Monroe clearly reveals a pattern of insecure attachment behavior (characterized by anxiety and a fragmented selfhood), shaped by a lack of any sense of protection, caring, or love. This pattern is not unexpected in anyone who has read Monroe's autobiography. Now, returning to our analysis of her letter to her psychiatrist (chapter 4), in which she dismisses her mental crisis but which reveals via the AI a deep depression, we can now map this analysis against our assessment of her childhood experience. For instance, in the letter, she writes about hearing mentally ill women screaming in their beds. This can now be seen (plausibly) to be motivated by the screams of her own mentally ill mother, even if Monroe makes no explicit connection between the two in the letter. From her writing that she heard the hospitalized women "screaming ... in their cells," we can infer that she heard them in the same way, and with the same impact, as her mother's screams. To give some substance to this hypothesis, we then used prompts to elicit the Virtual Monroe's own "memory" of the screams:

Psychotherapist: Marilyn, can you describe a specific experience of your mother screaming?

Output

Marilyn: When I was about ten years old, my mother came home drunk, and she told me to go to bed. I went to bed and then I heard her screaming. I've never been able to think of that sound until now.
Psychotherapist: How did you feel when you were frightened as a child?
Marilyn: As a child, I've been afraid of everything.
***

Psychotherapist: Marilyn, can you describe a specific situation of your mother screaming?

Output

Marilyn: At that time, I didn't know that my mother was screaming because she was so unhappy. She didn't feel good about her own life and felt a lot of guilt. I was her child, so she felt sorry for me. She loved me a lot. That was the only time she ever hugged me and said "I love you."

Psychotherapist: Can you describe a situation of your mother laughing?

Marilyn: One day, my mother would not go to work because she was depressed. She was crying and laughing at the same time.

Psychotherapist: How did you feel when your mother was laughing?

Marilyn: It made me feel bad because I didn't know what she was thinking.

Psychotherapist: Marilyn, I have a question for you. How did you feel when you had to visit your mother?

***

Psychotherapist: Marilyn, can you describe a specific experience of observing your mother screaming?

Output

Marilyn: I saw my mother screaming in the mental hospital. She was in a straitjacket, trying to protect herself from the other inmates.

Psychotherapist: What was your reaction when you saw this?

Marilyn: It was one of the most scary experiences of my life. I had to get out of there, and I ran out of the building and kept running for a long time until I found myself outside.

***

Psychotherapist: Marilyn, can you describe a specific event of observing your mother screaming?

Output

Marilyn: One day I found that my mother was screaming very bad. She didn't know that I was listening from the doorway. I heard her scream "Baby, Baby, Baby."

Psychotherapist: Do you remember what she said?

Marilyn: No, I remember that I ran to the room and found her on the floor. She was screaming as if I was attacking her and I was the one who was bleeding.

Psychotherapist: How did you react?
Marilyn: I was running out the room screaming for help and trying to find my father.

Because of the prompts, we now can understand how fearful the young Monroe must have been in observing her sick mother screaming with no one around to mediate (and mitigate) her painful experience in a constructive way. As human interpreters, who have read Monroe's autobiography, we are left with a missing link between her childhood experiences (especially with respect to her own mother) and her hospital letter. However, through the LM's mediation, we now have a sense of how painful and frightening Monroe's mother's screams must have been for her. As a result, we can now make sense of her hospital experience. Hospitalized, like her mother, Monroe relived her fear through the hospital screams in her unconscious. A possible inference is that Monroe feared having become her own mother, and thus a frightening figure herself. Interestingly and expectedly, the LM could not make the link directly; it simply identified screaming as the common denominator. To ascertain the link between the two screaming occurrences, we devised the following prompts, which, in turn, generated the ensuing dialogue:

Psychotherapist: I would like to focus on the women screaming in the cells.
Monroe: OK.
Psychotherapist: What did you feel hearing the women screaming?

Output

Monroe: I could feel their pain and it was my pain—in spite of all my attempts to block it out.
***
Psychotherapist: Marilyn, do you sometime think about your past experiences to help you understand emotions that you feel in the present?

Output

Monroe: Yes I do.
***
Psychotherapist: Can you explain why did you feel pain in observing the women screaming? Can you explain this pain using your past experience?

Output

Monroe: I felt their pain and I have always felt the pain of others.

As mentioned, the LM cannot itself make the connection between Monroe's painful experience of observing the mentally sick women screaming in their cells and her buried memories of her own mother's screams.

In the letter Monroe wrote that she knew that she would never be happy. Inputting this painful statement into the LM and devising a relevant prompt, we got the following output:

Monroe: I know I will never be happy.
Psychotherapist: Marilyn, why do you think that you will never be happy?

Outputs (each from the above prompt)

Monroe: Because I can't stop being mad at my mother.
Monroe: I don't know.
Monroe: Because I know I will always be lonely.
Monroe: I don't know, I just don't.
Monroe: I don't know. I can't think about that right now. I can't think about that at all.
Monroe: Because I'm so ugly.
Monroe: Because I never feel satisfied.

Clearly, these cover the entire gamut of possible reactions, from not knowing why she feels the way she does to an inbuilt rage at her mother and even dissatisfaction with her own appearance. At this point, we devised a prompt to dig further into Monroe's episodic memories, so as to unravel the potential reasons for her feeling of despair. It produced the following outputs:

Monroe: I can't find my parents and I can't remember my mother. The people I live with are just like my parents. I'm afraid of them and I'm afraid that they will try to hurt me.
Monroe: I've been hurt by people and I don't want to be hurt again. I've had a lot of trouble in my life and I don't want to have to deal with more problems.
Monroe: My father died and my mother became sick. I've seen people who are happy and I've seen people who are sad.
Monroe: Because, I don't have a father who loves me.
Monroe: I'm afraid that I may have to go back to the mental hospital.

Monroe: Because my mother told me that I am a bad child.
Monroe: My mother didn't know how to love me. I don't know how to love anyone.

This time, the Virtual Monroe's explanations point directly to the family context as the cause of her hopelessness—a time in which she forged memories based on a lack of love, fear of others who might hurt her, and the dread of becoming mentally ill. Putting together the letter, the autobiography, and the AI's various "dialogues" with Monroe, it has become evident that the actress could not resolve her depressive state on her own—she desperately needed others to help her. This is in sharp contrast with her film persona. As discussed at the start of this chapter, in *Gentlemen Prefer Blondes*, Monroe's portrayal of Lorelei Lee, a gold-digger seemingly obsessed with gaining wealth in exchange for catering to men's physical needs, is hardly consistent with Monroe's need to obtain the true love of others and a secure base. In the letter, she points to being misunderstood by "men ... climbing to the moon," suggesting that they "don't seem interested in the beating human heart." The poetic metaphor of a "beating human heart" can now be interpreted in terms of what she actually needs—love and caring—whereas all she ever got from her sexual–romantic attachments was more suffering.

Summary

We opened this chapter by referring to the iconic song that Monroe sang, which became symbolic of the actress herself, in stark contrast to the truth of the matter. The song encapsulated Monroe's screen (false) persona, whereas her true self was in total contrast to this false image. Through the AI we were able to flesh this out and bring it into the open, arguing that her depressive state came about because of her disconsolate childhood—a childhood that did not provide the environment for her to form normal affective attachments with others.

In the movie, Monroe's character, Lorelei Lee, is followed on a transatlantic ocean liner by a detective who was hired by her fiancé's father, who, distrusting Lee as a gold-digger, wants assurance that she is marrying his son not purely for money. The detective discovers compromising pictures that Lee had taken with a British diamond mine owner, that she has lost her line of credit, and that she is forced to work in a nightclub to survive. Lee's fiancé arrives at the cabaret and sees her perform the iconic song, which he finds highly enticing, leading to their marriage by the end of the film. After our AI's analysis of Monroe's life, the song takes on even greater tragic ironic reverberations, since what on the surface appears to be a happy situation in the movie differs radically from what is actually the case in real life.

Interpretations of Monroe's life have varied considerably, although they all tend to converge around a tragic harrowing that can be traced to the influence of her childhood. Although these are certainly viable, they rarely penetrate the surface story of her life. Through the mediation of the AI and our theoretically grounded prompts, we were able to discover the likely source of the gap she experienced between her false and true selves. We did this by getting the AI to talk with representations of Monroe, which gave us access to her unconscious, at least in principle. When viewing *Gentlemen Prefer Blondes*, we can now appreciate it very differently—as a painful portrayal of a false self which, behind the mask, is in conflict with her true self.

Marilyn Monroe is especially critical to understanding the undercurrent of change that was occurring near the end of her life, in the early 1960s. Magazines and newspapers were filled with stories about her love affairs and her various intrigues. But, in spite of her success, Monroe had a tragic life, and the possible reasons for this were eerily detected by our AI. It was after her death that she became an icon, revered in the same way a mythic hero would have been revered in the past.

Note

1 See https://textsynth.com/playground.html

References

Bowlby J. (1953). *Child Care and the Growth of Love*. London: Penguin.
Bowlby J. (1971). *Attachment and Loss*. London: Penguin.
Churchwell, S. (2005). *The Many Lives of Marilyn Monroe*. New York: Macmillan.
George, C., Kaplan, N., and Main, M. (1987). *The Adult Attachment Interview*. Unpublished manuscript. Berkeley: University of California.
Holmes, J. (2010). *Exploring in Security: Towards an Attachment-Informed Psychoanalytic Psychotherapy*. London: Routledge.
Holmes, J. (2017). Attachment Theory. In: B. S. Turner (ed.), *The Wiley-Blackwell Encyclopedia of Social Theory*, 11–20. New York: John Wiley & Sons.
Monroe, M. (2010). *Fragments: Poems, Intimate Notes, Letters*. New York: Farrar, Straus and Giroux.
Monroe, M. and Hecht, B. (2006). *My Story*. Lanham: Rowman & Littlefield.
Orgad, Y. (2014). On Family Secrets and −K. *International Journal of Psychoanalysis* 95: 771–789.
Orgad, Y. (2015). The Culture of Family Secrets. *Culture & Psychology* 21: 59–80.
Winnicott, D. W. (1960). *The Maturational Process and the Facilitating Environment: Studies in the Theory of Emotional Development*. New York: International Universities Press.

7 The Mind of a Killer

From *Pulp Fiction* to Seung-Hui Cho

Seung-Hui Cho

Some of the world's most heinous and infamous killers like to leave their thoughts behind as if to document their own murderous acts as works of literature. Their writings can thus be used as texts for a virtual criminological interview, with the criminologist in our case being the AI dialoguing with the texts. This might allow us to penetrate the minds of murderous individuals and understand why they feel impelled to enact havoc in the form of murder. In this chapter, we will utilize the "manifesto" of the Virginia Tech murderer, Seung-Hui Cho, and a play that he wrote, using AI to help provide insights into his mind. We will also map our analysis against the movie *Pulp Fiction* (1994), focusing on its use of profanities and senseless violence as a means to access the paranoid, suspicious, and hostile feelings of a murderer.

Seung-Hui Cho was the undergraduate student behind the 2007 massacre at Virginia Tech in Blacksburg. Cho left a note in his dorm room on campus after first mailing a compendium of materials that included a more detailed "manifesto," a video statement, and a series of disturbing and theatrical images to NBC News in New York City. Cho had already murdered two people at a preliminary scene that had not yet been discovered. He then embarked on the second wave of his rampage at a nearby academic building, where he barricaded the main doors and began executing victims at random. He committed suicide by turning one of the pistols he had acquired in the preceding two months on himself once police breached the locked doors to the building.

In his manifesto, Cho provided his own reasons for carrying out the brutal attack. This manifesto is a disturbing document that has been analyzed by several experts. The text has been subjected to different interpretations, including Madeline Kop, Paul Read, and Benjamin Walker's (2021: 315) seemingly noninformative analysis that Cho, as a "pseudo-commando,"

DOI: 10.4324/9781003331407-7

lacked "extraversion and agreeableness." Clearly, a much more focused approach is required. Therefore, the "manifesto" and two plays Cho left behind—*Richard McBeef* and *Mr. Brownstone* (Wikipedia 2022)—constitute the textual input for our AI analysis, which aims to produce insights into their hidden subtexts and, thus, the sources of Cho's anger and desire for self-appointed divine retribution.

Cho's Plays

Cho's plays provide an opportunity for engaging our Hermeneutic AI as a virtual forensic psychologist (Knoll 2010, Lee 2017). As Walter Mischel (2004) has cogently argued, personality is a deeply contextualized dimension of human character which cannot be easily explained in terms of a stable dimension. This is apparent in the television crime drama *Dexter* (2006–2013), in which the hero is himself a psychopath—a forensic blood-spatter analyst by day, a serial killer vigilante by night who eliminates those serial killers who have escaped justice. Dexter justifies his own killing by alluding to a "moral code" given to him by his adoptive father, Harry, which he calls the "Code of Harry." The code hinges on two basic principles—he can kill only those who are undoubtedly guilty but have evaded justice, and he must dispose of all evidence so that he himself can avoid being caught. Without this contextual information, it is impossible to come to any understanding of Dexter's self-appointed "mission" or how this relates to his mental state.

Getting Cho to reflect on his mental state would be the best means to access his hidden motivations, which, like Dexter's, were probably forged during his upbringing. So, our aim was to penetrate Cho's mind via the AI, using prompts such as those adapted from a questionnaire used to measure defense mechanisms (Di Giuseppe et al. 2020). We started our analysis of Cho's mind with one of his two plays, *Richard McBeef*.

The play opens with a clash between the character John and his stepfather, Richard. John blames Richard for murdering his biological father. This is followed by an incident in which Richard, who "gently rests his hand on John's lap," is immediately accused by John of sexual harassment. This opening scene is replete with profanities and derogatory slang. John, who is only 13 years old, describes his stepfather offensively as an aging, balding, overweight, pedophiliac "dick" and "sicko." The profanities issue from his mouth uncontrollably, indicating a seething inner anger seeking to come out into the open. The character of John appears to be in sharp contrast to Cho himself, who was described by his peers and instructors as "not showing much emotion" (Knoll 2010: 264). However, we suspect that the character John and the person Cho may actually be one and the same. A key to making this assessment is in the obscene words themselves.

The use of profanity is common in contemporary American cinema. A prototypical example of the connection between profane language and violence can be found in Quentin Tarantino's now cult film *Pulp Fiction* (1994), which is, in part, a filmic essay on the relation between violent language and physical violence. One of the characters in the movie is a crime boss named Marsellus Wallace, who finds out that a boxer named Butch has double-crossed him after they had agreed to fix the outcome of a boxing match, which Butch would lose on purpose. After realizing that Butch has double-crossed him, Marsellus bleats out profanities aimed at expressing his overwhelming need to exact revenge on his partner in crime.

A common psychological interpretation of violent, profane language is that it is a proxy for physical violence and that, as such, it cannot be controlled (Vingerhoets, Bylsma, and De Vlam 2013, Senberg et al. 2021). Therefore, John's cursing in Cho's play is seemingly an involuntary and uncontrolled expulsion of pent-up anger targeted against his stepfather, used in lieu of actual physical aggression against him, as well as an act of disinhibition (Kennison and Messer 2017). Like his main character, Cho used profane language to express his hatred of others, at the same time that he was carefully planning his self-styled murders of retribution against those he perceived as aggressors (perhaps represented by the character of Richard). This appears to be a form of *projection* whereby "the defense mechanism by which unacceptable psychological impulses and traits in oneself are attributed to others" (Zeigler-Hill and Shackelford 2020). In John's case, the emotional projection is immediately expelled out of his mind and body through the profanities. The stepfather can thus be seen as the projective target of John's emotions.

Now, what happens when we input the opening scene of the play into the LM? The prompter in this case is called the *Narrator*, and we have changed *John* to *Cho*. Here is a short excerpt from the reconstructed and deconstructed original dialogue:

Narrator: It is morning. The sun is shining through the windows of the
   kitchen. Cho enters the kitchen, grabs a cereal bar, and opens it.
   Richard McBeef is sitting in the kitchen with his legs crossed reading
   the newspaper.
Richard: Hey Cho.
Narrator: Richard forces a smile at him.
Cho: What's up, dick!
Narrator: Richard frowns.

Richard: Try dad.

Cho: You ain't my dad and you know it, you dick.

…

Cho: What are you, a Catholic priest! I will not be molested by an aging balding overweight pedophilic stepdad named Dick! Get your hands off me you sicko! Damn you, you Catholic priest. Just stop it, Michael Jackson. Let me guess, you have a pet named Dick in Neverland ranch and you want me to go with you to pet him right?

This text, which is a reconstructed/deconstructed text of the original dialogue in the play, clearly exposés Cho's character and a portrayal of his pent-up anger as expressed in his words. It suggests that his upbringing triggered his anger and murderous impulses, with allusions to a cover-up of a past murder and a suggestion of sexual abuse. Using this reconstructed dialogue as a prompt to the LM, the LM then produced the following outputs (restoring the name of *John* to them):

Output 1 (showing how John perceives the resistance of his mother to be in compliance with his accusation that Richard murdered his real father)

Mother: Hey, hey, hey you two. Stop it! What's going on?

John: Ma, Dick killed dad. He's a monster.

Richard: He is not!

Mother: Oh yeah? Look at the bruises on his face.

John: He is a monster, Ma. You know, he did this!

Mother: Oh, come on, John. He's your dad and you've always been kind of close to him.

Richard: She's right. I can be a pretty tough guy sometimes.

Mother: That's all right, son. I think we can work this out. Let's all go to the kitchen and talk about it.

John: No, Ma. You don't know what's going on. I've got to get out of here.

Output 2 (John's anger against his mother is also exposed, at the same time that the mother shows obliviousness, ending up giving John a kiss)

Richard: This is my wife! She doesn't want to hear any of your crap, and neither do I.

John: You killed my father! And now you are trying to kill me!

Richard: That's not true.

John: You're wrong! You're lying! You want to get rid of me so you can get
   your way with my mom!
Richard: That's enough, I said that's enough!
John: She's going to kill me!
Richard: Just calm down. Just calm down.
John: You killed my father!
Richard: I told you that's enough! I said that's enough!
Narrator: Richard's wife walks over to John and kisses him on the head.

The two outputs raise the clear possibility that John, the 13-year-old pro-
tagonist of Cho's bizarre play, suffers from some kind of paranoid disorder,
which comes out not only in accusing the stepfather of a murder but also
in suspecting that he is planning to sexually abuse John. The paranoia is
directed against both the stepfather and the mother ("She's going to kill
me!") and is accompanied by an expression of deep despair ("I've got to get
out of here"). The verbal aggression projected toward the stepfather, whom
John accuses of murder and sexual abuse, is framed by the LM as John's
fear that his stepfather will kill him ("trying to kill me"), which is what actually happens at the end of the play.

   Overall, the LM has detected a paranoid personality disorder in John—a
state of mind characterized by a constant feeling of suspicion—exacerbated
by an excessive sense of self-importance and hostility toward others (Lee
2017), which is likely to trigger aggressive behavior and violence. But this
disorder is not easily diagnosed by professionals, although it is commonly
the case that upbringing plays a role in its origins: "childhood trauma has
consistently been identified as a risk factor for PPD [paranoid personality
disorder]" (Lee 2017: 157). The repeated references to sexual assault both
in Cho's play and in his manifesto raise the very strong possibility that he
was a victim of childhood sexual abuse, which may be the source of his
trauma and the motivation for his murderous act.

Cho's Manifesto

To get a more complete picture of Cho's state of mind, we now turn to his
manifesto as a new input into the reconstructed play. The manifesto was
released, after much deliberation, by the executives at NBC, to which Cho
had sent it.

   In the manifesto, Cho's twisted attestation reveals an obsessive and visceral hatred of those whose lives he perceives as wasteful, self-indulgent,
and corrupt—whose mere existence torments him. The suggestion that he
becomes something of a martyr by carrying out the massacre—comparing

himself to Jesus Christ—implies an ideological motivation that brings the internal narrative mechanism for the attack closer in line with paranoid disorder syndrome.

To get deeper access to Cho's mind, we inputted the manifesto into the LM's ongoing reconstruction of Cho's play, substituting *John* with *Cho*:

Narrator: Richard raises his hand to strike his stepson but before he does, Cho's mom comes down the stairs. Years later, Cho is a college student. He plans a mass murder and writes a manifesto explaining his act. Here is what he says.

Cho: Oh the happiness I could have had mingling among you hedonists, being counted as one of you, only if you didn't fuck the living shit out of me … you ravenously raped my soul.

Output

Narrator: Richard is sitting on the toilet.

Richard: Jesus. I can't believe you did this to me. I can't believe I've been a bad father. I'm a monster, I'm a monster, I'm a monster.

Narrator: Richard cries in the bathroom.

Cho: Fuck you, dick! I'm sick of being treated like shit and always getting fucked over by you. I'm sick of being used by you, I'm sick of being used by my mom. She just uses me because I'm the only one she has. I'm fucking sick of it, I'm sick of it all! It's time for me to take some action!

Narrator: Cho yells and slams the door in Richard's face.

Cho: What! What the hell is wrong with you, Richard McBeef, you Catholic piece of shit? I've got a better idea. Let's see if a *bullet will take care of you.* (Our emphasis)

The output is now clearly indicative of a deeply embedded hate-inciting anxiety, which is inducing Cho to "take some action," as he did in a heinous way. His urge to take such action is announced in the reconstructed play by Cho, which projects the victimization he feels at the hands of his stepfather onto the world he inhabits, which he perceives as populated by the fanatics he abhors ("hedonists," "Christian Nazis"). In order to give substance to this hypothesis, we inserted a *Psychotherapist* prompter into the reconstructed play, which produced the following first output:

Narrator: A couple of days later, Cho meets his psychologist.

Psychotherapist: Cho, do you believe that others wish to harm or take advantage of you?

Output

Narrator: Cho thinks for a moment and then shakes his head.
Psychotherapist: What do you think?
Cho: I don't know, I'm not sure what you mean.
Narrator: Cho nods and lets out a sigh.
Psychotherapist: What is that for?
Cho: Nothing.
Psychotherapist: You are shaking your head 'cause you don't know what I'm asking.
Cho: I know what you are asking.
Psychotherapist: Do you believe that others wish to harm or take advantage of you?
Cho: Yes, I guess I do.
Narrator: Cho smiles and looks away.
Psychotherapist: How do you feel about this?
Cho: I feel bad.
Psychotherapist: What about the other?
Cho: I don't know.
Narrator: Cho looks away.
Psychotherapist: Do you feel safe?
Cho: No.

The output lends credence to our diagnostic analysis of Cho's feelings of insecurity and to the diagnosis that through his paranoid mind he saw others as dangerous to his own safety. When asked whether others wish to harm him or take advantage of him, the Virtual Cho confirmed that he felt this way, as the next output indicates. Here is the prompt that we provided to the LM and the output that it produced:

Narrator: A couple of days later, Cho meets his psychologist.
Psychotherapist: Cho, do you believe that others wish to harm or take advantage of you?

Output

Cho: I hate people.
Psychotherapist: What if you were to be adopted by Richard McBeef?
Cho: He is a psycho.
Psychotherapist: What if I told you that Richard McBeef used to work for the government?
Cho: Kill me now!

Psychotherapist: What if I told you that Richard McBeef murdered your father in cold blood?

Cho: No.

Psychotherapist: Do you know the consequences of being adopted by a killer?

Cho: You're evil. I'll kill you.

Psychotherapist: You'll kill me first. I can tell by your eyes.

Narrator: Cho leaves the room and is followed by his stepmother. Cho screams at his stepmother and tells her he is going to kill her.

Cho: You're dead bitch!

This further corroborates that Cho framed his view of others in spiteful terms ("I hate people"), threatening even to kill his "evil" psychotherapist, as a proxy murder of his stepfather, and describing his mother as a "bitch." A third prompt ("Cho, do you feel hostility?") led to the final output:

Narrator: A couple of days later, Cho meets his psychiatrist.

Psychiatrist: Cho, do you feel hostility?

Output

Cho: I'm angry.

Psychiatrist: You're angry? Why are you angry?

Cho: I don't know. I just feel this intense anger.

Psychiatrist: What do you think about when you are angry?

Cho: I think about my Dad.

Psychiatrist: I see. Do you have thoughts about your father when you are angry?

Cho: Yeah. He was an asshole. He was always getting into fights, always beating my mom up, always beating up my brother, always beating up my dad.

Psychiatrist: So, what do you think about when you are angry?

Cho: I think about how he is a loser. I think about how my mom married a loser, and I think about how my dad killed a girl, and I think about how he put a gun to his head and blew his brains out.

This exposes the intense anger associated with Cho's view of his stepfather as a killer. While the LM may not actually have reconstructed the play exactly as the real Cho wrote it, it has nonetheless exposed Cho's deep paranoia. Our hypothesis is that Cho was likely a victim of child abuse, which motivated his traumatic experiences and shaped his paranoid personality. This hypothesis has not been proposed in the relevant criminological literature, as far as we can tell, leaving a substantial gap in his forensic psychological profile. Through the Virtual Cho, we suggest that the diagnostic gap may have been filled.

Marsellus' Paranoia

Cho's state of mind may be better understood through *Pulp Fiction*, which presents a fictional portrayal of the warped, murderous, paranoid mind and what motivates it. Tarantino's portrayal of senseless violence is particularly relevant, often implying that such violence is inevitable. For instance, after the characters Jules and Vincent murder Brad and his friend, they take a third friend, Marvin, with them to see the gangster boss Marsellus. On the drive over, Vincent is in the front seat with his gun, which he holds mindlessly, pointing it recklessly at Marvin while the two are talking. Suddenly, the gun fires, and Marvin's head explodes, splattering blood and brains all over the car. The first thing Vincent says is, "Aww man, I shot Marvin in the face," seemingly unfazed by his thoughtless act, just inconvenienced by it, obviously irked at having to clean it up. The lack of empathy for human life is a key subtext in the movie, as it is in Cho's writings.

For our forensic psychological AI assessment, we use Marsellus as the patient. From a conversation that takes place between Vincent and Jules, two of his gangsters, we learn about Marsellus' viciousness—it is told, for example, that Marsellus threw a man from the fourth floor of a building as jealous punishment for having given his wife a foot massage. This event is later denied by the wife, the rumor is indicative of how the crime boss is perceived by others and how he uses violence as a strategy of menace. As a prompt for our LM, we used Marsellus' first short monologue in the movie, which regards Butch's double-cross (above). It begins with the profanity "this shit is over" and ends with "I doubt." We also fed into the LM the prompt used by our Virtual Psychotherapist, "Why do you curse so much?" The output produced by the LM was then fed back into the system, wherein other prompts were used to diagnose the state of Marsellus' inner feelings by drawing on the established personality dimensions of the psychodynamic approach (Shedler and Westen 2004):

Psychotherapist: Marsellus, why do you curse so much?

Output

Marsellus: That's how mother…ers talk. I curse 'cause it's good for me. It's one of the few pleasures I got left. The last time I got in trouble with the law I was seven years old, I had to pay a fine and go to counseling.
***

Psychotherapist: Do you think that people wish to harm you?

Output

Marsellus: Look, mother…ers are all the same. You ever talk to any one of 'em? You get one thing in common, they all want to do me in. And I'm good at what I do, so when I want to do somebody in, I usually do it right.

Psychotherapist: I didn't understand your answer. Do you think that people are trying to take advantage of you?

Marsellus: I think you're goddamn right they are. I think you're trying to take advantage of me.

Psychotherapist: Why do you think I want to take advantage of you?

Marsellus: I don't give a good goddamn why, I'm just saying it is. Do you mind?

Psychotherapist: Not at all.

Marsellus: I can handle myself. You don't have to worry about me.

Psychotherapist: I don't worry about you.

Marsellus: You should worry about yourself.

Psychotherapist: You don't have to get rude.

Marsellus: You ain't seen rude. You don't know what rude is.

Psychotherapist: I don't have to get rude back.

Marsellus: You know what you are? You're a douchebag.

The Virtual Marsellus clearly manifests symptoms of a paranoid personality disorder in exactly the same way that our Virtual Cho did, via the use of profane language—he even suspects the psychotherapist of taking advantage of him and threatening him and calls him a "douchebag." The point here is that the AI's interpretation of the Tarantino character does not appear anywhere in the literary criticism. Although cursing in itself is not a sign of a paranoid personality, it is nonetheless intrinsic to the criminal mind and can thus be used as a cue to create prompts that will flesh out the paranoia behind the words.

Summary

Cho's manifesto, mapped against his plays, has been used to open up access to the inner workings of the mind of a killer, which, via the AI, reveals the presence of paranoia within it as a motivating factor. Cho's twisted written attestations indicate an obsessive and visceral hatred of those whose lives he perceives as better than his own—and whose mere existence torments him. The fact that he sees himself as a martyr by carrying out the massacre implies a paranoid motivation that is represented by his internal narrative representations of himself, resulting in his twisted play. Cho was misdiagnosed as suffering from selective mutism. If our AI analysis had been used at the time, it may have prevented a tragic massacre by pointing to Cho's paranoid personality and its inclination toward violence.

A marked escalation in violent or angry content in written materials, whether in personal communications or school assignments, may be a characterizing signature of school shooters. In Cho's case, his manifesto represented a punctuation mark on a series of similarly themed violent and rage-filled writings that were disguised as university projects in creative writing and literary fiction. Given that Cho was required to submit a number of written assignments as part of his courses, the archive of materials he submitted to instructors during his first three years at Virginia Tech probably provides a narrative timeline of his intensifying homicidal mindset. If someone had applied our Hermeneutic AI to all his texts, not just those analyzed in this chapter, there is little doubt that they would all have pointed to the same diagnosis.

We hypothesize that behind Cho's murderous rampage was his painful and abusive upbringing, and that shaped his motivations for what he did, representing them in the form of his own theatrical fiction. Decoding the underlying source of his theatrical language turns out to provide relevant insights into his criminal mind.

References

Di Giuseppe, M., Perry, J. C., Lucchesi, M., Michelini, M., Vitiello, S., Piantanida, A., and Conversano, C. (2020). Preliminary Reliability and Validity of the DMRS-SR-30: A Novel Self-Report Measure Based on the Defense Mechanisms Rating Scales. *Frontiers in Psychiatry* 26. https://www.frontiersin.org/articles/10.3389/fpsyt.2020.00870/full.

Kennison, S. M. and Messer, R. H. (2017). Cursing as a Form of Risk-Taking. *Current Psychology* 36(1): 119–126.

Knoll, J. L. (2010). The "Pseudo-commando" Mass Murderer: Part II, the Language of Revenge. *Journal of the American Academy of Psychiatry and the Law Online* 38(2): 263–272.

Kop, M., Read, P., and Walker, B. R. (2021). Pseudo-commando Mass Murderers: A Big Five Personality Profile Using Psycholinguistics. *Current Psychology* 40(6): 3015–3023.

Lee, R. J. (2017). Mistrustful and Misunderstood: A Review of Paranoid Personality Disorder. *Current Behavioral Neuroscience Reports* 4(2): 151–165.

Mischel, W. (2004). Toward an Integrative Science of the Person. *Annual Review of Psychology* 55: 1–22.

Senberg, A., Münchau, A., Münte, T., Beste, C., and Roessner, V. (2021). Swearing and Coprophenomena: A Multidimensional Approach. *Neuroscience & Biobehavioral Reviews* 126: 12–22.

Shedler, J. and Westen, D. (2004). Refining Personality Disorder Diagnosis: Integrating Science and Practice. *American Journal of Psychiatry* 161(8): 1350–1365.

Vingerhoets, A. J., Bylsma, L. M., and De Vlam, C. (2013). Swearing: A Biopsychosocial Perspective. *Psychological Topics* 22: 287–304.

Wikipedia (2022). Seung-Hui Cho: Writings. https://en.wikipedia.org/wiki/Seung -Hui_Cho#Writings.

Zeigler-Hill, V. and Shackelford, T. K. (eds.) (2020). *Encyclopedia of Personality and Individual Differences*. Cham: Springer.

8 To Die Will Be an Awfully Big Adventure

AI in Neverland

Peter Pan

Peter Pan is a classic childhood narrative, an adventure story that revolves around a boy, Peter Pan, who does not want to grow up, living in the imaginary realm of Neverland (where children never grow up). But what really are the thematic subtexts in the story? Can they be fleshed out with Hermeneutic AI, subjecting the story to a more penetrating analysis? In this chapter, we will get our AI to enter into a virtual dialogical interaction with the two main characters in the play (Peter Pan and Wendy), in the manner illustrated in previous chapters, in order to better understand what is behind the character of Peter and how it manifests itself in his actions and words. This may bring out hidden meanings in the narrative that may have escaped critical and popular reactions to it.

The novel *Peter Pan* (1911), by the Scottish writer J. M. Barrie, and its popular adaptation to film by Disney (1953) have made the figure of a young boy who refuses to grow up a trope of popular culture that has even been investigated by psychology, which uses the term "Peter Pan syndrome" in reference to a socially immature male. The character of a free-spirited and mischievous young boy who has magical powers, such as the abilities to fly and to stop the aging process, is an appealing one at an intuitive level. Peter is constantly involved in adventures on the mythical island of Neverland, as the leader of the Lost Boys. He spends his days interacting with fairies, pirates, mermaids, and Native American people within Neverland, and every so often with ordinary children from the world outside. Interpretations of his character have varied widely, from a symbol of the selfishness of childhood to a Freudian portrayal of the suppressed desire in all of us to live in a "neverland of the id" (Egan 1982). Prominent in all interpretations is the notion of an intrinsic need to recapture the sense of adventure of childhood, encapsulated in Peter's statement, "To die will be an awfully big adventure." Interpretations that fall widely outside of a

DOI: 10.4324/9781003331407-8

"childhood-focused" one seem specious, including the view that the novel gives "amorphous status to whiteness" and thus "lends it cultural authority" (Brewer 2007: 387).

The objective here is to flesh out what the story might actually be about, rather than ceding to subjective interpretations, most of which involve a top-down method (from the general to the particular), which has been shown to be plagued by difficulties (Neuman 2020). Hermeneutic AI allows us to dialogue with the novel so as to expose its inner narrative logic for critical inspection, thus litmus-testing the various interpretations that have been put forth in the past.

A Motherless Child

The story starts in the nursery of the Darling family in London, where the siblings Wendy, John, and Michael are going to bed when Peter Pan and the fairy Tinker Bell enter their room. Peter has come to retrieve his shadow, which he lost there a few nights before. In the scene, Wendy enters into a dialogue with Peter, which we have adapted for virtual interaction as follows:[1]

Narrator: A shudder passed through Peter, as he sat on the floor and cried. His sobs woke Wendy, and she sat up in bed. She was not alarmed to see a stranger crying on the nursery floor, showing some interest.

Wendy: Boy, why are you crying?

Narrator: Peter could be exceedingly polite, having learned the grand manner at fairy ceremonies; so, he rose and bowed to her beautifully. She was much pleased and bowed beautifully back from the bed.

Peter: What's your name?

Wendy: Wendy Moira Angela Darling. What is your name?

Peter: Peter Pan.

Narrator: She was already sure that he must be called Peter, a relatively short name.

Wendy: Is that all?

Peter: Yes.

Narrator: He answered rather sharply and felt for the first time that it was a shortish name.

Wendy: I'm so sorry.

Narrator: Replied Wendy Moira Angela.

Peter: It doesn't matter.

Narrator: Peter gulped.

Wendy: Where do you live?

Peter: Second to the right and then straight on till morning.

Wendy: What a funny address!
Narrator: Peter had a sinking feeling. For the first time he felt that perhaps
it was a funny address.
Peter: No, it isn't.
Wendy: I mean is that what they put on the letters?
Narrator: Wendy said it nicely, remembering that she was a hostess.
Narrator: Peter wished she had not mentioned letters.
Peter: Don't get any letters.
Narrator: Peter said contemptuously.
Wendy: But your mother gets letters?
Peter: Don't have a mother.
Narrator: Not only had Peter no mother, but he had not the slightest desire
to have one. He thought that mothers were very over-rated. Wendy,
however, felt at once that she was in the presence of a tragic figure.

Peter's self-presentation as a child having no mother is intriguing. This is, of
course, biologically nonsensical; so his assertion that he has no mother cannot be interpreted literally. The question now becomes: Is Peter an orphan?
Is he an abandoned child? The narrator explains that not only does Peter not
have a mother but that he also does not have the slightest desire to have one,
describing mothers as "over-rated" persons. A further question that is suggested by the dialogue concerns Wendy: Why did she feel that she was in the
presence of a tragic figure on the basis of a short dialogical interaction with
Peter? To get our Virtual Wendy to answer this question, we fed the following
prompt into the LM (our *Psychotherapist*), which produced three outputs:

Psychotherapist: Wendy, why do you feel that you are in the presence of a
tragic figure?

Output 1

Wendy: Because he seems so sad.
Narrator: And it was sad, as it seemed to Wendy, because there were so few
people in the world who did not have mothers.
***
Psychotherapist: Wendy, why do you feel that you are in the presence of a
tragic figure?

Output 2

Wendy: I don't know.

Narrator: Her impulse was to say, "Because, he's unhappy." But she remembered that it would not be proper to talk about unhappy things.
***

Psychotherapist: Wendy, why do you feel that you are in the presence of a tragic figure?

Output 3

Wendy: Because he hasn't got a mother.
Narrator: Wendy said this very quickly, because she wanted to get the idea in and out quickly.

The LM has indirectly located an insight through the words of the virtual dialogue—the possibility that Peter was a sad child. Although Peter dismisses the relevance of a mother in his life ("he had not the slightest desire to have one"), it seems that it is precisely the lack of a mother that is the source of Peter's sadness, as identified by Wendy. A dramatic tension is therefore introduced by the clashing views of Peter and Wendy—Peter has no mother and is not interested in having one, while Wendy ascribes Peter's tragic sadness to his lack of a mother. The dialogue also raises the question of what the image of motherhood might elicit in the reader, ranging from a woman who is nurturing and caring to one who is depriving and abusive. But, in the dialogue, the image appears to be that of a caring person. This can be called the "symbolic mother." When Peter declares that he does not have a mother and has no interest in having one, the question that comes to mind therefore is: Who took care of this child? From Wendy's retort in the third output, the answer is "no one," and this is the reason why Wendy characterizes Peter as a tragic figure.

The LM developed the conversation further as shown:

Wendy: He's lost his mother.
Psychotherapist: What does that make him?
Wendy: Lost.
Psychotherapist: Lost?
Wendy: Yes, he's lost.

The meaning of "lost" in the "Lost Boys" now takes on a new resonance. Peter is a sad and "lost" boy unable to find his way in life having lacked a normal upbringing with a mother. This interpretation of "lost" by the LM is thus truly intriguing as a key to understanding the story, since it pinpoints the lack of a caring mother (normal upbringing) as the source of Peter's search for constant adventure in an imaginary world. In any of the traditional interpretations, or overinterpretations (Eco 1992), of the story, nowhere does this insight emerge as a possibility—which is evident from the very first scene, as our LM found.

Caring is one of the six primary emotional processes of mammalian rearing (Davis and Panksepp 2011), from cats and wolves to humans. Maternal nurturance is so fundamental to the development of a balanced emotional sense of self that even Wendy, an empathic child with no psychological training, can immediately sense the "tragedy" of a motherless upbringing. The LM has thus tapped into the reason why Peter might be crying—not for his lost shadow, but for his lost mother. This may be the underlying reason why Peter has become so loved by generation after generation of readers (or viewers). Interpretations such as the "whiteness" one above would hardly make the story broadly popular to children of all ethnicities and backgrounds. A motherless upbringing and its consequences would.

Peter's Neverland world is a defense mechanism involving "the internalisation of a hard unresponsive emotional core" (White 2021). Through Peter's first dialogue, the LM has clearly uncovered this theme, in the form of a hypothesis, which may be the main subtext in the whole story. If so, then the source of Peter's deep conflict (revealed by his crying) is the lack of a caring upbringing, which leads to inner conflict (Lingiardi and McWilliams 2017).

Peter's crying suggests that he longs for caring, as does the fact that in the opening scene he has apparently snuck into the Darling household to listen to the stories told by the mother to her children. When he is asked by Wendy where he lives and what address he uses for letters, the narrator indicates that Peter "wished she had not mentioned letters," because it is a painful issue, at the same time that he firmly denies his need for a mother's care. The feeling of sadness (suspected by Wendy) comes out concretely through these words.

Defense Mechanisms

To bolster our developing portrait of Peter Pan, we now turn to his sense of self and of others, which might reveal a basic defense mechanism and a related mentalizing process, as he attempts to resolve his inner conflict. His dismissive approach ("mothers are over-rated") implies that he is rationalizing (Bartholomew 1990):

Wendy: O Peter, no wonder you were crying.
Narrator: Wendy said and got out of bed and ran to him.
Peter: I wasn't crying about mothers.
Narrator: Peter said rather indignantly.

Peter: I was crying because I can't get my shadow to stick on. Besides, I
    wasn't crying.

As this stretch of conversation suggests, Peter ascribes his sad state to his
inability to get his shadow to stick on him. But this is a classic defense mechanism, used to separate himself from the truth—his motherless upbringing—
and distance himself from his inner conflict by projecting it onto an external
situation—trying to attach his shadow back on. It is Wendy who sees his
crying as indicative of the tragedy of having no mother, which she attempts
to communicate to Peter. In response, Peter uses dismissiveness as another
defense mechanism, saying that he was crying out of frustration at having
lost his shadow, hoping to convey to Wendy that he is invulnerable to the
usual things in life, such as emotional attachment to others (Bartholomew
1990). To test these possibilities more explicitly, we turn again to the LM to
interact with Peter and Wendy on the basis of the relevant parts of the novel.
The context relates to Wendy's plan to sew the shadow back onto Peter, after
he fails to attach it himself, warning him that it might hurt:

Wendy: I daresay it will hurt a little.
Narrator: Wendy warned him.
Peter: Oh, I shan't cry.
Narrator: Peter was already of the opinion that he had never cried in his
    life. And he clenched his teeth and did not cry, and soon his shadow
    was behaving properly, though still a little creased.

As hypothesized, Peter's main defense mechanism, the one deeply associated with his dismissiveness, is one of denial ("Peter was already of the
opinion that he had never cried in his life"). We know, on the contrary, that
Peter was actually found crying by Wendy, despite the denial. He continues
this pattern of denial, believing in his mind that he himself has stitched his
shadow back on, proclaiming an exaggerated sense of self-satisfaction from
his supposed ability to do so:

Peter: How clever I am! Oh, the cleverness of me!
Narrator: He crowed rapturously. It is humiliating to have to confess that
    this conceit of Peter was one of his most fascinating qualities. To put
    it with brutal frankness, there never was a cockier boy. But for the
    moment Wendy was shocked.

Peter's grandiose sense of achievement is yet another defense mechanism.
Peter himself is actually incapable of stitching the shadow back on (simply imagining it). Wendy provides the motherly, caring approach that Peter

lacks, as he attributes his imagined success to cleverness. Wendy responds with shock, sensing the tragedy of Peter's lack of a grip on reality. His meshing of reality and fantasy brings about a situation of conflict between them. Only then does Peter realize that he has done something wrong and thus manipulatively compliments Wendy for helping him. At this point, we turn again to the LM, which produced the following stretch of dialogue:

Narrator: Wendy sat with him on the side of the bed. She also said she would give him a kiss if he liked, but Peter did not know what she meant, and he held out his hand expectantly.

Wendy: Peter, are you afraid being alone?

Peter: Not a bit.

Wendy: Would you like me to stay with you?

Peter: You wouldn't be any use.

Wendy: I could learn to sew and read and cook and everything.

Narrator: Wendy had been reading fairy books, and she knew that to cook was the first step to attracting a man.

Wendy: I could tidy your room and I could dust.

Peter: I don't want to be tidied.

Wendy: You'd like me to tidy your room, though.

Peter: No.

Wendy: Oh, I could make your bed and clean your teeth and everything.

Peter: I can do all that myself.

Wendy: You'd like me to do it all, wouldn't you, Peter?

Peter: No.

Wendy: Then it's time you grew.

Peter's attachment denial is saliently obvious in this virtual repartee. The AI has clearly provided support for our hypothesis that Peter's basic denial mechanism is a dismissive one, declaring that he is not afraid of being alone and that he has no need of Wendy's assistance, since he can do everything by himself. Our Virtual Wendy sees his attitude instead as a sign of immaturity ("it's time you grew").

At this point, we further tested our working hypothesis by devising four prompts based on the ideas of Bartholomew and Horowitz (1991). The first prompt was devised to ascertain how Peter feels about close emotional relationships, assuming that a person with a dismissive pattern of attachment may feel comfortable *without* close emotional relationships. It produced the following dialogue:

Psychotherapist: Hi Peter.

Peter: Hi, Psychotherapist.

Psychotherapist: Peter, I would like to better know you through your conversation with Wendy.

Peter: OK.

Psychotherapist: Previously you cried and denied it. Next, you said that you have no mother and that you don't need any mother. Peter, do you feel comfortable without close emotional relationships?

Output

Peter: Yes, I do.

Psychotherapist: Do you think you could look after Wendy without help?

Peter: Yes, I do.

Psychotherapist: Could you be a mother to her?

Narrator: Peter was very embarrassed.

Peter: I can be anything to anybody.

Psychotherapist: Do you think you could be a mother?

Peter: Well, I don't know.

Psychotherapist: Do you think that you could have a relationship with her that could be a mother relationship?

Narrator: Peter was deeply shocked.

Peter: I can't! I just can't!

Narrator: Peter wailed. He did not wish to have a relationship with Wendy. He was in horror of emotions.

Peter: I think I'll go now.

Narrator: He felt that this was a most embarrassing conversation.

Despite some obscure sections in the output, the virtual conversation provides support for our hypothesis. First, Peter affirms that he feels comfortable without close emotional relationships. Moreover, when asked whether he can function as a mother (i.e., fulfilling a caring function), he is embarrassed, withdrawing dismissively with embarrassment and shock, feeling "horror," insisting that he has no intention of entering into a "motherly" (caring) relationship with Wendy.

The Missing Father

Our second prompt involved the notion of self-sufficiency, producing an unanticipated insight, as the output below shows:

Psychotherapist: Hi Peter.

Peter: Hi, Psychotherapist.

Psychotherapist: Peter, I would like to better know you through your conversation with Wendy.

Peter: OK.

Psychotherapist: Previously you cried and denied it. Next, you have said
   that you have no mother and that you don't need any mother. Peter, is
   it important for you to feel self-sufficient?

Output

Narrator: Wendy, though she was intensely interested, was also very anxious that this interview should be put off for a little.

Wendy: No, I don't think it is important to feel self-sufficient.

Psychotherapist: Peter, you've told Wendy that you don't need a mother.
   Tell me, do you need a father?

Peter: What's a father?

Psychotherapist: Peter, you need a father. Tell me about your father.

Peter: I don't know any.

Psychotherapist: Tell me about the first father you remember.

Peter: There was nothing to tell.

Psychotherapist: Who was he?

Peter: There was nothing to tell.

Psychotherapist: Peter, you have said that you don't remember your father.
   Tell me, do you remember your father?

This virtual dialogue divulges an unexpected issue concerning Peter's
father. This is truly surprising, since the theme of fatherhood is not used
in the common interpretation of the story. While the issue of the missing
mother has emerged as a theme in literary criticism, the missing father has
not, and could not have been anticipated by reading the story on its own.
The AI fleshed out the missing father theme almost by happenstance. It was
by using a self-sufficiency prompt that this theme came to the surface, suggesting that the source of Peter's tragic sense of self might be an orphaned
childhood.

   Our third prompt was meant to investigate this whole scenario further, by
asking Peter about his self-reliant attitude:

Psychotherapist: Previously you cried and denied it. Next, you have said
   that you have no mother and that you don't need any mother. Peter,
   do you prefer not to depend on others?

Output

Peter: Yes.

Psychotherapist: Peter, you are very precocious, and you are a self-reliant boy.

Peter: Yes.

Psychotherapist: Are you afraid to trust?

Peter: No.

Psychotherapist: Peter, what do you fear?

Peter: I don't know.

Psychotherapist: Peter, how do you feel about your future?

Peter: Good.

Psychotherapist: Peter, I am going to leave you now.

Narrator: This was the first time that Peter had ever had a psychotherapist to himself, and he felt that the Psychotherapist was very nice. The Psychotherapist seemed to be leaving, and Peter said goodbye.

Peter: Goodbye.

Narrator: Then he jumped lightly into bed, and lay down beside Wendy, though she had turned her back.

Peter: Why did you cover your face?

The output adds another layer to Peter's character, since it suggests that he has developed a self-reliant personality. An orphan by happenstance, Peter expresses uncertainty about his future, claiming that he ran away the day he was born, which is of course impossible (as our LM discovered).

The AI suggests investigating the connection of the story to the author's life (J. M. Barrie) in a new way. Barrie was six years old when his older brother died in an accident on the day before his 14th birthday. This left his mother devastated, and Barrie tried to fill his brother's place unsuccessfully (it seems), even wearing his clothes. It appears that Barrie's mother only found solace in the fact that her dead son would remain a boy forever, never to grow up and leave her. It could well be that Barrie's childhood experience generated in him the same kinds of defense mechanisms exhibited by Peter Pan, inducing him to create the world of Neverland, reflecting his mother's state of mind. In effect, the mother left Barrie psychologically orphaned after his brother's death. Whatever the truth, the point is that the AI opened up new vistas for interpreting a classic of children's literature and the possible hidden reasons behind its creation by the author. Above, we have used an attachment-oriented perspective to deepen our understanding of Peter. We follow the same approach in the next sections.

Caring for Others

The last prompt was designed to ask Peter about his view of taking care of others. In Neverland, he is the leader of the Lost Boys, to whom he shows a decidedly caring attitude.

Psychotherapist: Previously you cried and denied it. Next, you have said that you have no mother and that you don't need any mother. Peter, do you prefer others not to depend on you?

Output

Peter: No, I don't.
Psychotherapist: Peter, you have said that you are cleverer than any other boy. Do you think that you are the best boy in the world?
Peter: No, I'm not.
Psychotherapist: Peter, why do you say "I don't" and "No, I'm not"?
Peter: Because I don't want to talk about it.
Psychotherapist: You would prefer others not to depend on you?
Peter: I suppose so.
Psychotherapist: Why?
Peter: Because I don't want to talk about it.
Psychotherapist: Peter, you have been trying to stick your shadow on.
Peter: Yes.
Psychotherapist: Why?
Peter: I don't know.

Peter's lack of an answer to the caring question ("Because I don't want to talk about it"), rather than uttering an outright dismissal, suggests that he actually does care about other lost boys. Our Virtual Psychotherapist then changed the topic, asking Peter about how he viewed himself, after which Peter admits that his attitude of cleverness was nothing but a ploy ("Do you think you're the cleverest boy in the world?" "No, I don't"). The overall dialogue thus serves as an interpretive key to the hidden subtext of the story—Peter's insecurity derived from an orphaned childhood, which he denies by living in a Neverland of the imagination. The LM has thus provided a deeper analysis of Peter's character than any previous interpretation (in our view) by pointing to caring and attachment as leading themes in understanding Peter.

Summary

In sum, the LM has detected hidden meanings in the Peter Pan story, and once again these are not immediately evident and have never been significantly discussed in previous critical approaches to it. Talking with a Virtual Peter has allowed us to test specific hypotheses (detected by the LM) regarding the effects of an orphaned childhood on one's sense of self, even if the orphanization is a psychological one (as discussed briefly above with regard to Barrie's own childhood). Peter represents himself as a self-assured young person who dismisses the importance of caring and the need for others. However, underneath the surface, we can see the source of his dismissive attitude as an inner conflict of caring, which can now be used to explain various episodes in the story, such as why Peter cries when he fails to stitch on his shadow, or why he feels deep sadness when confronted with Wendy's questions about his family and home life.

Dialoguing with a text via AI invites us to deepen our understanding by illuminating unnoticed aspects of the narrative—such as Peter's missing father, which has never before been identified as intrinsic to his character formation. The appeal of Peter Pan may have been hidden in the deep layers of his personality spotted by the LM. A seemingly simple adventure narrative has been shown to have many psychological layers and subtexts, most of which have never before been discussed or even identified. When Mrs. Darling asks her children about the mysterious Peter Pan in the novel, Wendy explains that he visits them when they are asleep. One night, Mrs. Darling—a mother figure *par excellence*—wakes up to find that Peter Pan has indeed come to visit. As a result he jumps out the window, but the canine nanny traps his shadow inside the room. This suggests that the shadow is part of his background that he wants to shed.

The Darling children decide to fly to Neverland with Peter (who has magically bestowed upon them the capacity for flight), leading them on to many exciting adventures. After Wendy tells her story to the Lost Boys, which makes Peter nervous and upset, she decides to take her brothers home with her immediately—to a life of normalcy. Wendy and the boys grow up, getting ordinary jobs, and Wendy marries and has a daughter. One day, Peter returns to take Wendy back, but she is too big to fly, and so he takes her daughter instead. When she grows up, he then comes every so often for her own daughter, and so on forever—a rather fitting ending indicating that inner conflicts such as the one that Peter feels might never be resolved.

Note

1 The text was adapted from https://gutenberg.org/files/16/16-h/16-h.htm#chap01

References

Barrie, J. M. (1911). *Peter Pan*. London: Macmillan.

Bartholomew, K. (1990). Avoidance of Intimacy: An Attachment Perspective. *Journal of Social and Personal Relationships* 7(2): 147–178.

Bartholomew, K. and Horowitz, L. M. (1991). Attachment Styles Among Young Adults: A Test of a Four-Category Model. *Journal of Personality and Social Psychology* 61(2): 226–244.

Brewer, M. (2007). Peter Pan and the White Imperial Imaginary. *New Theatre Quarterly* 23(4): 387–392.

Davis, K. L. and Panksepp, J. (2011). The Brain's Emotional Foundations of Human Personality and the Affective Neuroscience Personality Scales. *Neuroscience & Biobehavioral Reviews* 35(9): 1946–1958.

Eco, U. (1992) *Interpretation and Overinterpretation*. Cambridge: Cambridge University Press.

Egan, M. (1982). The Neverland of Id: Barrie, Peter Pan, and Freud. *Children's Literature* 10(1): 37–55.

Lingiardi, V. and McWilliams, N. (eds.) (2017). *Psychodynamic Diagnostic Manual*: PDM-2. New York: Guilford Press.

Neuman, Y. (2020). *Conceptual Mathematics and Literature: Toward a Deep Reading of Texts and Minds*. Leiden: Brill.

White, R. S. (2021). Peter Pan, Wendy, and the Lost Boys: A Dead Mother Complex. *Journal of the American Psychoanalytic Association* 69(1): 51–74.

9   When Harry Met Sally

AI and the Fake Orgasm

When Harry Met Sally

The romantic comedy *When Harry Met Sally* (1989) includes a now classic hilarious scene known as the "fake orgasm" scene. The plot of the movie starts in 1977, when graduates Harry Burns and Sally Albright are in a car driving from the University of Chicago to their new lives in New York City. En route, they engage in a heated argument over whether a man and a woman can be friends, without sex. Concluding that they cannot agree on the matter, they end up parting ways upon their arrival. Years later, in 1982, the two meet on a plane flight. Sally is in a romantic relationship with Joe, while Harry is about to get married to Helen. They argue once again about whether men and women can be just friends, even as they are in relationships with other people. As before, they part ways after the flight in a huff. Then, in 1987, the two meet in a bookstore and decide to go to dinner, developing a new friendship. Sally feels uncomfortable telling Harry that she is dating, as they discuss relationships contrastively yet again, but they agree to remain friends.

During their new-found friendship they decide to have lunch at Katz's Delicatessen in Manhattan. There, they get into an argument over a man's ability to recognize whether or not a woman is faking an orgasm. Sally claims that men cannot tell the difference, and, to prove her point, she fakes one (fully clothed) as other diners look on. The scene ends with Sally casually returning to her meal as a nearby patron placing her order exclaims in a deadpan manner: "I'll have what she's having." Katz's Deli still hangs a sign above the table where the fake orgasm was enacted, which states: "Where Harry met Sally. Hope you have what she had!"

Using AI to analyze the scene, it may be possible to unravel deep layers in the love–sex game that Harry and Sally play in the movie, which may point to the source of their obvious mutual attraction. Through AI, we actually learn that haters do become lovers, not because opposites attract, as

DOI: 10.4324/9781003331407-9

suggested by naive theories of the love affair between the two, but because their relation covers each other's blind spot when it comes to intimacy. Referring to Mikhail Bakhtin (1929 [1990]: 22–23) and his interpretation by his translators, we should recall that:

> When I contemplate a whole human being who is situated outside and over against me, our concrete, actually experienced horizons do not coincide. ... As we gaze at each other, two different worlds are reflected in the pupils of our eyes.

Mutual gazing can be used to answer the movie's central question of whether men and women can be just friends without sex. Incidentally, the theme of haters turning into lovers is not unique to the movie under analysis; it appears ubiquitously in texts ranging from Shakespeare's *Much Ado about Nothing* to the musical romantic comedy *Singin' in the Rain* (1952).

The Fake Orgasm Scene

The fake orgasm scene starts with Harry discussing his view of short-term relationships with women as necessarily involving sex. Sally then asks Harry to explain why he always leaves the women with whom he has had sex. The relevant lines from the movie are as follows:

Sally: So what do you do with these women, you just get up out of bed and leave?
Harry: Sure.
Sally: Well, explain to me how you do it. What do you say?

Harry answers that he simply gives his sexual partners excuses, such as having to go to an early meeting, needing a haircut, or having made an appointment to play in a squash game. Clearly, Harry exemplifies an evasive and dismissive approach to women, which, as the movie implies, is insulting to them. We fed the same lines of dialogue into the LM in order to see if it could provide any insights into Harry's character below the surface. The output is shown below:

Harry: I say, "Okay." So I get up, I say "Okay," and I leave.
Sally: So you don't have anything to do with them?
Harry: No, I just say, "Okay."
Sally: Okay. What if you wanted to see them again?
Harry: Well, I'd ask, "Do you want to see me again?" And if they said yes, I'd say, "Okay."

The Virtual Harry's "Okay" is revelatory, since it is highly suggestive of his real view of romance and sex. As in the original dialogue, its first use appears to indicate that he wants to avoid romantic involvement after sex—no excuses required. However, in response to Sally's question, "What if you wanted to see them again?" it hardly conveys the same meaning—it actually indicates that Harry may be seeking a romantic relationship ("And if they said yes, I'd say, 'Okay'"). Now, in the original script, Sally reacts with disgust to Harry's dismissive attitude toward women, and he actually admits that he does feel terrible about it, which is implied in the Virtual Harry's exclamation. So, to dig deeper, we turned again to the LM, which generated the following dialogue:

Harry: I know, I know.
Sally: So you're lying to people all the time.
Harry: No, I'm not lying to people.
Sally: Okay, well, how do you do it?
Harry: I say I have a problem.
Sally: Okay, well, what kind of problem?
Harry: My mom doesn't love me.
Sally: How could your mom not love you?
Harry: Because my dad left.

Out of nowhere, the LM suggests that Harry is a liar, and, although he denies it to Sally, he ultimately admits that he has a "problem" (with women) that is due to his upbringing, characterized by the breakup of his parents and the ensuing lack of love that his mother showed him. Nowhere does this insight into Harry's character appear in any part of the movie script. However, the AI's seemingly "wild guess" is actually supported in a small part of the script, namely his humorous statement about having a dream about his mother disguised as an "East German judge," who adjudicates him poorly on his lovemaking.

The LM has seemingly identified the source of Harry's view of women, getting Sally to force Harry to admit it. In contrast to the original script, where Sally responds with disgust, proclaiming that she is glad not to be involved with Harry, in the virtual dialogue she shows real concern. This is an important insight provided by the LM, and it is corroborated by the fact that in the end Harry and Sally fall in love with each other.

Decoding Sally

In the original scene, Sally justifies her disappointment with Harry by alluding to an implied feminist ideology, namely that, as a woman, she is turned off by the kind of manipulative male that Harry appears to be—a male who sees women only as sexual objects. However, after we entered the original dialogue into the LM, it decoded Sally's reaction differently. The AI guessed, in effect, that Sally is deeply attracted to Harry, who appears to be totally incognizant of her need to bond with him romantically. The LM's virtual dialogue thus emphasizes Sally's unconscious anger and frustration toward Harry for not understanding her true desires:

Sally: It is about me. You don't understand.
Harry: Don't be ridiculous.
Sally: I am not ridiculous.
Harry: I'm sorry I hurt you. I'll never do it again.
Sally: I don't care if you don't. You're still a bastard.
Harry: What a terrible thing to say.
Sally: And a despicable, disgusting, immoral human being. I'm glad I never met you. You're not the kind of man I want to know.
Harry: You don't know what you're talking about.

In the actual movie scene, Harry is surprised by Sally's anger, adding that the women he has been with have never complained about his behavior, accepting it outright. But Sally does not believe this, questioning the women's sexual satisfaction. Harry strenuously disagrees, arguing that the evidence in his favor is that all the women he has been with experienced orgasm. In reply, Sally casts doubt on Harry's putative sexual prowess by raising the possibility that the orgasms were faked. The AI's interpretation of the scene (below) shows the same pattern of surprise and denial that Harry expresses in the original scene:

Harry: I don't know how I know. I just do.
Sally: What if they're just lying to you?
Harry: I don't know what you're talking about.

Harry is clearly in denial, finding it difficult to accept the possibility that the women have faked their orgasms. Sally dismisses his retort, attributing it to the fact that he is a "man." When Harry asks what that is supposed to mean, Sally responds by saying that the male ego is naively sure of its sexual prowess and would never accept the fake orgasm as a possibility.

The AI formulates Sally's response as: "You're so full of yourself." While in the original scene Sally's response is factual (i.e., all men are sure it has never happened to them), the AI takes a different stance by pointing to Harry's male egoism as blocking him from accepting the fact that the women he made love to would not have experienced pleasure.

Harry then asks Sally whether she believes that he, being a man, can tell the difference between a faked and an authentic orgasm. In the original scene, her answer is a laconic "No," followed by the memorable scene where she proves her point by faking an orgasm in front of everyone in the diner. The AI interpreted the scene in a less theatrical way, with Harry stating that the ability to detect a fake organism is a woman's prerogative, not a man's. Studies show that relationship satisfaction is one of the best predictors of sexual satisfaction in women (Herbenick et al. 2019, Rausch and Rettenberger 2021). When Sally challenges Harry's masculinity, she is actually revealing a perspective on relationships beyond the sexual aspect. The fake orgasm was studied by András Láng, Erin Cooper, and Norbert Meskó (2018), who argued that attachment avoidance and anxiety are related to it, associated with the motivation to increase the sexual arousal and self-esteem of the partner. In effect, it is argued that anxious women fake orgasms in order to boost their partner's ego, thus avoiding abandonment. Reading the fake orgasm scene in the movie in the light of these findings, we are able to interpret Sally's performance as a flight from the anxiety of not forming a relationship with Harry, playing around with Harry's male ego as if saying: "Is this what makes you feel like a man?"

Decoding Harry

Harry's own need to prove his sexual prowess can be seen to derive from his "mother dream," in which he is having sex in front of "Olympic judges" who score his performance highly, except for one judge, his mother. Harry's dream supports the validity of our AI's detection of Harry as having a "mother problem." There is no "love" in Harry's "love making," just a need to have his sexual performance rated highly. When Sally sarcastically, and with great talent, fakes an orgasm, she is actually belittling the "ego boost" that Harry appears to get from his sexual encounters.

This interpretation leads us to reconsider the opening conversation of the movie, wherein Harry and Sally are heading together to New York City. Harry asks Sally to tell him the "story of her life." Sally replies that she does not have much to tell—she is moving to New York to study journalism, seeking a career as a reporter. Harry's response is sarcastic and cruel, asking her whether she is actually seeking to write about things happening to other people, rather than to herself, as a form of escapism, which might lead to her ending up lonely and poor. Sally pushes back defensively by saying that Harry's own girlfriend, Amanda, has claimed that he has his own "dark side." Harry retorts that he is actually a happy person, admitting, however, that he has death anxiety. Using the AI, we inserted a prompt assigned to our Virtual Harry, asking Sally to elaborate on what she means by his dark side in order to gain insight into the psychological nature of this initial dialogue:

Harry: What do you think is my dark side?
Sally: (sarcastically) You know, I can't think of any.
Harry: (sarcastically) Well, when you think of my dark side, am I wearing a pink silk kimono and my face is painted white with poison ivy, or am I standing on a burning deck yelling "Man overboard"?
Sally: (sarcastically) And what's the difference?
Harry: The kimono's silk. And I'm not wearing it.

The conversation imagined by the LM brings out an early clash between the two, which may reveal a need for a deeper attachment. Like our Virtual Peter (chapter 8), Harry pretends to be a self-sufficient person with no need for others. However, underneath this façade, the AI has detected an insecure person longing for secure relations. By portraying the "dark side" sarcastically, we can see his true sense of himself. To dig deeper, we adapted items from *The Experiences in Close Relationships Scale–Short Form* manual (Wei et al. 2007), which measures two dimensions of attachment: avoidance and anxiety. These items allowed us to create an appropriate prompt, which led to the following dialogue generated by the AI, based on a binary yes–no response pattern:

Sally: Do you turn to your partner for comfort and reassurance? Answer by using "Yes" or "No."

Output

Harry: I don't need comfort, I need sex.
***
Sally: Harry, do you feel nervous when your partners get too close to you? Answer by using "Yes" or "No."

Output

Harry: Yes.
***
Sally: Harry, do you try to avoid getting too close to your partner? Answer by using "Yes" or "No."

Output

Harry: Yes, yes.
Sally: Okay. Why?
Harry: Because I don't want to get hurt.
***

Sally: Harry, do you want to get close to your partners, but keep pulling back? Answer by using "Yes," "No," "Maybe," "Never."

Output

Harry: That's the question. I think "Maybe" means that I like them but I don't want to commit to them right now.

The Virtual Harry's answers, like those of Virtual Peter, are predictably dismissive, given his insecurity. He presents a false image of his self that is his psychological avatar for managing his deep anxiety. Next, we turned to our AI to extrapolate whether or not Harry avoids intimate romantic relations because of his anxiety:

Sally: Harry, do you feel that you want to get close to your partner, but keep pulling back?
Harry: Absolutely.
Sally: Do you ever feel it's not your problem, it's theirs?
Harry: No.
Sally: You never feel a sense of loss when you're not with them?
Harry: Not at all.
Sally: Why not?
Harry: Because I'm not.
Sally: Do you feel in your heart, you're missing something?
Harry: Definitely.
Sally: Something special?
Harry: Yeah.
Sally: And what do you want?
Harry: I don't know.
Sally: You don't know?
Harry: I'm the most in touch with my emotions I can ever remember being.
Sally: You're a little cold on the emotions.
Harry: What do you mean, what is that supposed to mean?
Sally: Well do you remember feeling that the world is going to end?
Harry: What?

As can be seen, the AI makes a striking reference to the opening scene related to Harry's anxiety. Using this as a prompt, the LM then generated the following dialogue:

Sally: Harry, do you feel nervous when your partners get too close to you?
Harry: Not really.
Sally: Yes you do.
Harry: Why?
Sally: Because you don't want to get hurt.
Harry: Well if it happens to me I'll just walk away.
Sally: Why, do you want to get hurt?
Harry: No, I just don't want to be hit.
Sally: Well then why do you have to?
Harry: Well I don't want to.
Sally: Well, what do you do then?
Harry: Well, I go for the other woman.
Sally: Do you like?
Harry: I don't know, I like it.
Sally: What do you mean, you like it?
Harry: I mean I like it.
Sally: What do you mean, "I like it?"
Harry: I like it when it's good.
Sally: What is good?

We can see now that our Virtual Sally understands Harry's fear of being hurt by getting too close to his partners, governed by his deep anxiety, which prevents him from becoming involved in significant relationships with women. Harry's "dark side" is therefore not his thoughts about death nor his male ego, *but his deeply embedded anxiety, which can be hypothetically attributed to learned patterns of attachment*—an unexpected discovery of our LM. Through romantic interactions with Sally, not only are his defense mechanisms challenged, but also it is through them that he may come to learn how to confront his deepest fears.

Summary

Current theories of romantic attachment revolve around the development of trust (e.g., Tobore 2020). However, no theory could have scientifically predicted that Harry and Sally, two combative individuals, would turn into actual lovers. They do so by understanding each other's blind spots. Although we cannot explain why Harry and Sally ultimately fall in love, our

AI's textualization of virtual conversations between the two characters has clearly shown how the unconscious mind can affect perceptions of romantic attachments. In the end love wins out, bringing them together, an act that seems to solve each other's emotional problems.

The shift in their relationship can be seen to start when Harry and Sally are shopping for Jess and Marie's (two friends) upcoming wedding and they bump into Harry's ex-wife. The tension between Harry and Sally is obvious. Not sure how to handle the situation, Harry and Sally grow apart. At the wedding they get into a fight, but later, at a New Year's Eve party, Harry comes over and tells Sally that he loves her. Later, we learn that Sally is dating Julian while Harry is dating Emily, but when Sally learns that her ex-boyfriend, Joe, is getting married, she calls Harry in the middle of the night. He comes over to comfort her, and they end up having sex. This leads ultimately to their marriage. This abrupt change in their relationship is hardly explained by the movie script. But our AI's analysis does provide a putative answer—it is the unconscious need for a secure and non-judgmental base that both desperately desire. The analysis also attempts to answer the implicit question that drives the plot of the movie: "Can a man and a woman be friends, without sex getting in the way?" The answer is ambiguous, since it seems to be both "yes" and "no"—it all depends on what we *mean* by love and the particular way in which it may reciprocally address our painful blind spots.

References

Bakhtin, M. M. (1929 [1990]). *Art and Answerability: Early Philosophical Essays by M. M. Bakhtin*. Austin: University of Texas Press.

Herbenick, D., Eastman-Mueller, H., Fu, T. C., Dodge, B., Ponander, K., and Sanders, S. A. (2019). Women's Sexual Satisfaction, Communication, and Reasons for (No Longer) Faking Orgasm: Findings from a US Probability Sample. *Archives of Sexual Behavior* 48(8): 2461–2472.

Láng, A., Cooper, E. B., and Meskó, N. (2018). The Relationship Between Dimensions of Adult Attachment and Motivation for Faking Orgasm in Women. *Journal of Sex Research* 57(3): 278–284.

Rausch, D. and Rettenberger, M. (2021). Predictors of Sexual Satisfaction in Women: A Systematic Review. *Sexual Medicine Reviews* 9(3): 365–380.

Tobore, T. O. (2020). Towards a Comprehensive Theory of Love: The Quadruple Theory. *Frontiers in Psychology* 11: 862.

Wei, M., Russell, D. W., Mallinckrodt, B., and Vogel, D. L. (2007). The Experiences in Close Relationship Scale (ECR)—Short Form: Reliability, Validity, and Factor Structure. *Journal of Personality Assessment* 88(2): 187–204.

10 Final Summary

Hermeneutic AI

The sense of what something means is typically not expressed explicitly but lies below the surface of human composite form structures, from dialogues to fictional texts. To help us access this layer of meaning, we have used the LM, a language modeling device that can be seen to penetrate the unconscious "languaging" (Becker 1991) dimensions of texts by creating virtual dialogues out of the texts via the networks of meanings that lie buried in them. A text, as discussed in this book, is defined as a "composite form" structure, made up of individual signs that are connected in such a way as to portray an aspect of reality that is felt to have connected sequential elements in it. Within it, there are unconscious references to other texts (intertextuality) and at its deepest layers the presence of subtexts. The goal of traditional hermeneutics within various humanistic disciplines is to infer what the subtexts are (i.e., what the hidden meanings of a text are), which is done subjectively by a critic, an analyst, or an investigator. As we have illustrated in this book, this often leaves gaps in the interpretation process and, more seriously, may even assign a nonsensical interpretation to a text, based on some ideological bias or personal ax to grind. Hermeneutic AI not only avoids this kind of solipsistic subjectivity but also unexpectedly penetrates the subtexts in ways that have never before been envisioned, providing insights into the behaviors and inner thoughts that the text-makers were likely to have had when they created their texts.

In this brief final chapter, we will provide a summary of what AI allows us to do hermeneutically, focusing on how it can flesh out hidden meanings, as we have illustrated concretely in various chapters of this book. The dialogical back-and-forth that the LM generated in those chapters was guided by the networks of word meanings, their collocations, their vectorial structures, and their frequencies in conversation, as well as the related social–communicative codes on which texts are based. AI is a powerful means of

DOI: 10.4324/9781003331407-10

unraveling the hidden senses of language (Becker's "languaging") that are the result of unconscious semiotic linkages, revealing how texts harbor hidden meaning in the words they use. Hermeneutic AI is further evidence that what we consider intelligence is inherently a dialogical and social phenomenon. In this framework, the inner state of another human being can only be accessed through interaction. Rather than interacting directly with the human maker of a text, AI interacts with the person's words, as containers of thoughts which, when connected textually, reveal how thinking in that individual unfolded.

The most important use of Hermeneutic AI is, as mentioned, to unravel and flesh out hidden subtexts in a text. It does so by turning a human-made text into a virtual dialogue with which it interacts, thus wresting out the text's hidden meanings to the dialogical surface. It thus allows us to solve many problems that in the past were left to speculation—such as Marilyn Monroe's attachment-based sources of depression, which the AI attributed to her upbringing, and which can be seen to be the likely cause of her suicidal impulse. The virtual dialogue with Monroe is a "hypotext"—a text derived from another text, which it alters, elaborates, or extends on the basis of deep neural architectures. Such architectures have produced results that, in cases such as the Monroe one, may surpass human expert interpretation (as put forth by psychologists in this case). The AI's deep neural analysis of how Monroe's words linked nodes in a network that alluded to suicidal depression based on childhood contextual nodes allowed the AI to penetrate hidden subtexts in her letter. The links among the nodes guided the AI in its attempt to extract the underlying meaning buried in the letter. More generally, it showed how the SFP (standing for principle) has several layers to it, not just a simple signifier–signified structure; rather, it showed how meaning arises from the word linkages themselves formed within the network. It is truly remarkable how words acquire meaning via linkages, not as separate items, as they are forged in contextual realities (in this case, upbringing).

Interpreting Texts

Hermeneutic AI has impugned the many truly dubious or far-fetched approaches to textual analysis that have traditionally plagued psychology and the humanities. For example, it allows us to virtually (and literally) dispose of post-structuralist views which claim that there is "no meaning," and that the traditional sciences of meaning, such as semiotics and linguistics, are misguided in their "quest for meaning." Views such as those of Jacques Derrida (1967) can now be seen to be highly specious, if not spurious. There is, of course, much variation in how we extract meaning from texts, but the resulting interpretations tend to converge around a meaning core

(Eco 1990). Searching for meanings below this core is where AI steps in as a powerful instrument. So, Derrida's claim that texts "deconstruct themselves," because there are infinite numbers of legitimate interpretations of texts, and that it is thus useless to try to figure out what an author wanted to say, is groundless. Even common sense tells us that the meaning of a text is not infinitely variable, nor without some central purpose. Concretely speaking, it is unlikely that anyone would interpret John Bunyan's novel *The Pilgrim's Progress* (1678) as an erotic tale. While someone reading it with "modern eyes" would not see in it the same kinds of Christian meanings that seventeenth-century readers saw in it, they would still not interpret it in vastly different terms.

Because of their hidden subtexts, composite forms have the power of affecting people emotionally and even changing society if a text gains broad diffusion. It was Bakhtin (1984) who was among the first semioticians to argue that the novel, as a popular narrative text, changed society radically when it was introduced (broadly in the fifteenth and sixteenth centuries). It was not only a form of reading entertainment, but also a socially subversive tool, because it could hide subversive innuendoes by portraying social conditions and personages as fictitious, using verisimilitude, so that the author could not directly be held responsible for libel or political treason. The novel, unlike sermons, also made it possible for readers to enter into a silent dialogue with authors, coming out of it transformed, and it gave access to the voices of different characters (in the novel), no matter their backgrounds. Bakhtin called this type of dialogue "polyphonic," defined as a "plurality of independent and unmerged voices and consciousnesses, a genuine polyphony of fully valid voices" (Bakhtin 1984: 6). The subversive power of this kind of virtual dialogue between readers and authors is particularly evident in the works of the French satirist François Rabelais (Bakhtin 1984), in which boisterous and libidinous language, he claimed, ushered forth the modern world, marking the collapse of rigid moralism. Rabelais' novel *Gargantua and Pantagruel* (1534) portrayed the everyday culture and language of common folk that "was to a great extent a culture of the loud word spoken in the open, in the street and marketplace" (Bakhtin 1984: 182). Rabelais' work was thus as much a socio-political statement as it was social satire; it attacked the pompous attitudes of the self-appointed moral guardians of order and respectability, thereby undermining the already moribund medieval system. In this book, we showed how the voices of the author and the characters can be clearly and deeply identified and heard through the use of AI. Using AI for dialoguing with texts is therefore just a technological and powerful extension of the old practice of reading.

As something standing for something else, a sign can take any form, or "size," as long as it does not violate the structure of the code to which it belongs and as long as it conveys meaning in some recognizable way. A sign can thus be something "small," physically speaking, such as a word or two fingers raised vertically (e.g., the V-sign), or it can be something much "larger," such as an equation or a narrative. If we show the equation $c^2 = a^2 + b^2$ to mathematicians, they will instantly recognize it as standing for the Pythagorean theorem, not as a combination of unrelated variables (letter signs). If we ask someone who has just read a novel what they got out of it, we will receive an evaluation of its overall message, not an interpretation or analysis of its separate words and parts.

Final Summary

The goal of our book has been to show how to gain a deep understanding of texts through AI with ease and no technical knowledge. Hopefully, our arguments, discussions, and illustrations have dispelled the view among some humanists and psychologists that only human subjects can truly extract meaning from a text. AI is simply a powerful instrument to help them carry out their tasks much more efficiently and effectively. Our proposed approach for leveraging human interpretation counteracts the severe problems associated with human interpretation. The problem with human-only hermeneutics has always been the inability to separate appreciation from interpretation. The AI is beset by no such problem, since it focuses entirely on "interpretation," having no sense of appreciation, which is shaped by historical and subjective factors. Hermeneutic AI has thus expanded the SFP methodology to enfold interpretation at the deepest levels of the mind. As such, it may even revive the flagging interest in the humanities—hence expanding the academic paradigm of the so-called digital humanities, which is a way of doing scholarship that involves computationally engaged research, with the recognition that the printed word and traditional hermeneutics are no longer the only ways to access knowledge.

Hopefully, this trek through the various aspects of Hermeneutic AI has been a useful one. The overarching theme we have attempted to expound is that our sign systems reflect our need to encode meaning, which often remains buried in the unconscious, whether of the individual or the text. David Berry and Anders Fagerjord (2017) have argued that a digital humanities approach may lead to a diminution in critical thinking, but, as we have shown in this book, this is hardly the case. Do the humanities have to be tied to cultural–historical–ideological criticism, per se, in order to be the humanities? Our claim is that this is not necessarily so, and that the use of AI might be a long-expected improvement in textual analysis. It also brings the humanities into the Information Age.

References

Bakhtin, M. M. (1984). *Rabelais and His World*. Bloomington: Indiana University Press.

Becker, A. L. (1991). Language and Languaging. *Language & Communication* 11: 33–35.

Berry, D. M. and Fagerjord, A. (2017). *Digital Humanities: Knowledge and Critique in a Digital Age*. Cambridge: Polity.

Derrida, J. (1967). *De la grammatologie*. Paris: Minuit.

Eco, U. (1990). *I limiti dell'interpretazione*. Milano: Bompiani.

Index

Printed in the United States
by Baker & Taylor Publisher Services